Vivian French

ROOSTER BINGO

AND OTHER MOSTLY TRUE STORIES

ROOSTER BINGO

AND OTHER MOSTLY TRUE STORIES

by
Jerry Thompson

Rutledge Hill Press
NASHVILLE, TENNESSEE 37210

Copyright © 1987 Jerry Thompson

Published in Nashville, Tennessee, by Rutledge Hill Press, Inc., 513 Third Avenue South, Nashville, Tennessee 37210

Library of Congress Cataloging-in-Publication Data

1 2 3 4 5 6 7 8—92 91 90 89 88 87

Manufactured in the United States of America

I dedicate this book to you, my loyal readers, who have repeatedly urged me to publish a collection of my columns. Thank you. This book is for you.

Contents

Who? Me? Write a Book?

When *The Tennessean*'s publisher, John Seigenthaler, first said he wanted me to write a daily column, I hesitated. I had been a nuts-and-bolts reporter for almost a quarter-century, trying to write the facts, one after the other, so people who read them could understand what I had found out and why I thought it was important. I left the fancy writing and fanciful opinions to the lace curtain journalists who like to say words like *relevant* and talk about "macro-economics."

"What," I asked, "do you think I could write about?"

"About 750 words every day," he answered.

"But," I asked, "do readers of *The Tennessean* give a hoot about what an old country boy like me thinks about anything?"

He responded in predictable fashion, answering one question with two. "Are you intimidated by the idea? Do you have an inferiority complex about your opinions?"

His concept of motivation was about as hot as his sense of humor.

When I asked what I could write about every day, he merely said, "Think about it."

So I thought about it, and I discovered plenty. People I know, and people I don't know. Some I don't want to know. Places I've been, and places I haven't been. And places I wish my publisher would send me.

Almost every day there's something in the news I find interesting, and plenty I don't. Unusual things are blown out of proportion, and others, more ordinary, are ignored but shouldn't be.

Opinions? Oh, I don't spend much time with my chin on my fist contemplating, but my parents have never been accused of raising a dummy. They taught me common, ordinary horse sense. I know the difference, for instance, between that and what politicians pass off as horse sense. You have to scrape the latter off your shoe with a stick.

I began my columns with some of the things I like.

I like hot weather and cold beer.

I like to work in the garden. I like to plant seeds and watch them grow, full-blown, into flowers or vegetables.

I like to walk in the woods, through a park, or in a field. I like the smell of the outdoors whatever the season. And I like the smell of a kitchen, whatever meal is in the oven or on the stove.

I like to fish, even if I catch nothing. I like to play golf, but it's more play than golf with me.

I like children still small, playing and giggling, unaware of any threat. There is plenty of time later for them to worry about war, the economy, and prejudice.

I like mystery novels and history, writing, gin before dinner, wine with dinner, and brandy afterward. I like old people who talk about the past and good stories with punch lines. I like friends who know when to talk and when to shut up.

But there are things I don't like, too.

I don't like cold weather, and I don't like warm beer. I hate cold weather, but I don't hate warm beer. I feel about it about the same way I feel about halitosis: it's better than no breath at all.

I don't like preachers who talk about the Almighty as if they were God's hearing aid, or as if Jesus was theirs. I don't feel about them the way I feel about halitosis and warm beer. There are lots of good preachers. But better no preachers than those who get whispered messages that tell them what to say and do, or—worse—tell them what I ought to say and do.

I don't like dishonest people. I'm not talking about tellers of tall tales. We need creative story tellers. And I'm not even talking about monumental liars. We even need some of them. What would politics be without them? The dishonest people I don't like are the venal hustlers and con-game operators who deceive their fellow humans and don't care if they injure other people.

I don't like late phone calls or early morning appointments. I don't like mowing grass or Limburger cheese; I've got doubts about those who do.

I don't like jogging. I don't like to talk about jogging, and I don't like to read about jogging. Personally, I would prefer to be sick when I die.

I don't like mean husbands or wives who embarrass their spouses in public.

I don't like potholes in the street, sunburn on my legs, dirty dishes in the sink, books on how to improve your sex life, crying drunks, or dirty gossip.

These are some of the likes and dislikes that have pretty much guided my writing. What I've selected here are columns from "Thompson's Station" that look at what I like and dislike and try to find the humor in them.

From memories of boyhood and family to the experience of being a husband and father, from personal observations on life to the maddening irritations and silly ironies of the modern world, from true saints to the religious hustlers, this book is filled with stories of people I have known. Life today can be maddening, but if one is willing to look at it with a light heart, it can be extremely rewarding. It's that combination I have sought to capture in selecting these stories.

So welcome to *Rooster Bingo and Other Mostly True Stories*. I hope you enjoy reading it as much as I enjoyed its writing.

ROOSTER BINGO

AND OTHER MOSTLY TRUE STORIES

PART ONE

It Began with My Family

1

Mischief Never Asks "Why?"

Recently I found my shampoo bottle under the edge of the couch.

I had left it in the upstairs shower. The shampoo was gone, and the bottle had been refilled with water. Joe had struck again.

"Why did you do this, Joe?" I asked. "That bottle was half full."

"I don't know, Daddy," Joe answered.

My father, who happened to be visiting at the time, spoke up. "Don't ever ask a kid why they do things," he said. "You should know better than that. Joe's telling the truth. I'll bet he doesn't know.

"And furthermore, why did you throw ol' Blondie on my naked back?"

I instinctively ducked and looked for a place to run. That happened 35 years ago, and it was the first time Dad had ever mentioned it to me. He was calm. He made no quick moves toward me. And I noticed the left side of his face wasn't twitching.

"What did Daddy do, Granddaddy?" Joe asked.

"He'll tell you about it, Joe," said my father. "I guess I'll be going home now."

After Dad left, Joe kept badgering me to tell him what happened. I finally decided to tell him. I figured he should know it was only my fleetness of foot that allowed me to reach adulthood.

It was a hot, muggy Saturday morning. We were building a new house. Dad, who was doing most of the work himself on weekends, was dressed in cut-off jeans and tennis shoes and was down in the basement laying blocks for a partition.

The foundation blocks were just above ground level, making the basement about eight feet deep. My job was to place blocks in a crude V-shaped trough and slide them down to the basement level as Dad needed them.

As he bent over the mortar board, the sweat glistened on his naked back. I noticed ol' Blondie sunning on the blocks of the basement wall. Blondie was the meanest, most cantankerous, grouchy, biggest, old yellow tomcat I've ever seen.

To this very day I don't know why I suddenly picked ol' Blondie up and tossed him over the wall. I do know that he landed on his feet, all four of them with outstretched claws, right in the middle of Dad's naked back.

Immediately, awful sounds began coming from the basement. Blondie was screeching and clawing his way up the block trough. Dad was bellowing and trying to claw his way up the side of the basement wall; and he was shouting some real serious swear words with other words like *cat*, *kid*, and *kill* all mixed in.

For the life of me, I'll never know why, when ol' Blondie reached the top of the block trough, I slapped him back down into the basement. More dust flying. More awful sounds. This time it was Dad coming up the block trough. You have to understand that all this happened in less than three seconds.

I rapidly fled the premises. As I passed the third house down the road, I could still hear the plop of tennis shoes hitting the gravel road behind me. But the plops were growing fainter. I could also still hear such words as *cat*, *kid* and *kill*, but they also were more distant.

I didn't return home until almost dark, and when I did I was never more than a few inches from my mother.

After that day, whenever ol' Blondie would walk through the room, Dad would stop talking in mid-sentence, or quit whatever he was reading, and the whole left side of his face would go into a nervous twitch. That condition finally cleared up the next spring.

My brother Ronnie says he once heard Dad tell this story and that Dad actually laughed while telling it. Of course, I had left home and was married by then, and I never heard him mention it.

That is, until the other day when I ducked and looked for a place to run. And I'm positive I felt a twitch in the left side of my face.

2

The Preacher Got More Than Dinner

Parents are, by nature, a worried lot. Kids make sure they keep worrying.

Some of the things my brothers and sisters and I did, our parents could laugh about later. Others, they never found humorous.

One of my mother's biggest worries of all time, was how Ronnie and I, and even Dad, would act when the preacher came to supper.

It was part of a country preacher's pay that got him a free meal in the neighborhood every Sunday. And during revivals, the visiting preacher would come to the neighborhood in the afternoon and visit with the family that was to feed him that particular night.

You could always tell where the preacher had supper because he and the family always arrived at church at the same time.

When it was mother's turn to feed the preacher during revival, she had a little more than a week to get everything ready. At first, everything went smoothly. She was concentrating a little more on the routine cleaning and concentrating a lot more on our manners, mainly Ronnie's and mine. Our younger brother and twin sisters were too young to present much of a problem.

As the time grew nearer, mother became more serious. She seemed to lose her sense of humor. She almost fainted when Dad joked that he planned to tell the preacher he was eating out of Blondie's dish. Blondie was our cat. The rest of us laughed. Not mother.

She constantly tutored Ronnie and me, mostly on what we were not to do and say. "Whatever you do," she warned, "don't use any of the language you hear your daddy use. And whatever you do, don't take the preacher down to the old well."

The old well was where Dad washed out beer bottles before he refilled them with his own special home brew.

"Maybe you boys could say the blessing together," mother suggested. "We'll pick one you'll like and then we'll practice doing it together."

"I've got one," I volunteered. "Joe Crockett Shelton taught it to me.

"Bless the meat and damn the skin, open up and cram it in. Amen."

I got a good belly laugh going before her hand caught me across the mouth. I'd never seen mother so edgy.

Finally, the big day arrived. The house was all cleaned. The kitchen was filled with the aroma of fried chicken and fresh-baked pies. Excitement was in the air. Mother was nervous.

The preacher arrived earlier than expected. Much earlier than mother had hoped. She suggested that Ronnie and I might entertain him while she put the finishing touches on supper. Dad hadn't got home from work yet.

"Wanna go down to the old well?" were the first words to escape Ronnie's mouth. Mother rushed to the kitchen. The preacher seemed to enjoy Ronnie's explanation of the finer points of home brew.

"The top makes a loud pop when daddy opens the bottle," Ronnie said, "and blue smoke comes out."

Finally we settled around the table. Ronnie was just hitting full stride. Mother had the foresight to ask the preacher to say grace. Then Ronnie spoke up again:

"Daddy, will you open a bottle of home brew for . . ." Before he could finish the sentence, it was obvious Dad was kicking for him under the table. Dad made contact, but Ronnie got it out. Ronnie wanted the preacher to see the smoke and hear the pop.

Dad admitted later he made solid contact with his kick.

After that crisis, Ronnie spoke to the preacher:

"You know why ol' Blondie is looking at you like that?"

Mother gasped. Daddy kicked. This time much harder than before. It got results, too. The preacher yelped like a hit dog.

After profuse apologies, and a few nervous giggles, the preacher assured us he understood.

For years, mother said it was God's compassion that kept the other church members from asking about the preacher's new limp.

3

Grandmother Could
Keep a Secret

Now that I am past 40, I find that often some passing scene that never would have caught my attention a few years ago now triggers some memory from the past—even from childhood.

So it was the other day as I drove from the farm to the office. The sight of kids along the roadside picking up aluminum cans, salvaging them for recycling, brought back the memory of my wise grandmother who taught me never, never, never to waste anything.

Great Mama, as she came to be known as her great-grandchildren started coming along, had a saying for everything.

When a relative over 80 married a lady in her 20s, she mused, "There's no fool like an old fool—unless it's a young fool." That said what all my relatives were thinking about the newlyweds. It took Great Mama to give it expression.

As to waste, she saved everything. If she were alive today, I'm sure there would be tears in her eyes at what we waste. She would have wept over the food left on plates while people starve all over the world.

"Waste not, want not," she would say.

Everything had value to her. Not long ago I was in the supermarket and the fellow in front of me dropped a coin as he took his change from the cashier.

"Let it go," he said as I stooped to retrieve it for him. "It's just a penny."

Waste not, want not. I pocketed the coin.

Great Mama was a pioneer in recycling. She turned flour sacks into dish cloths and table cloths; she turned wild buck bushes into lawn sweepers. She saved pieces of string, peanut butter jars, plastic bags, bread wrappers and snuff boxes. Waste not, want not.

Were she alive today she would have praised the aluminum industry which several years ago began recycling aluminum products. The program has been so successful that the industry is now flooded with recyclable products. It has caused the price of scrap metal to drop from 40 cents a pound to less than 25 cents a pound.

Once I get to remembering Great Mama, I think not only of her wisdom but her tremendous sense of quiet humor. I recall the time when my little brother Ronnie and I flagrantly disobeyed our parents by taking out the .22 rifle and shooting at sundry targets while waiting for the school bus.

Our parents already had left for work. Our grandparents lived next door. We spotted an old red rooster pecking away in the backyard, well out of range of the rifle. There was no way we could hit him.

It was my turn to shoot. I hit him. One dead rooster. And two scared boys.

The consequences of shooting the rifle and killing the rooster were well known to us. Our backsides would be as red as the rooster by nightfall, unless we could come up with a story.

So we told our grandmother that we had seen the old sow run the rooster into the fence. It had broken the rooster's neck. We sorrowfully presented the dead bird to her. We knew it would make a wonderful dinner.

"Waste not, want not," said Ronnie.

Dinner at her house that night was wonderful. Baked chicken and dressing. We loved devouring the evidence of our crime. Our parents were not suspicious. But as we left her house that night, Great Mama took me and Ronnie aside.

"If I were you boys," she said, "I would watch that old sow."

"Why?" we asked in unison.

"She didn't break that rooster's neck," said our grandmother. "She shot him with a rifle."

She was no fool, that sweet, smiling, secret-keeping woman.

"There is no fool like an old fool," she might have said that night just to set up the punch line. "Except two young fools." And she loved them both. And they loved her.

4

Uncle Will's "Medicine" Packed a Wallop

If story telling is an art—and I, for one, think it is—my father is an artist. I think it comes from a God-given talent, helped along by a rich background of experience.

He has been a hotel bell hop, a prize fighter, a truck driver, a plumber, a glass blower, a hypodermic syringe maker, a service station attendant, a welder and—as he would say—several other less memorable occupations.

He courted my mother only six weeks before marrying her. He told Linda recently that it was such a short courtship because all his friends were telling her wild stories about him, and he had to marry her before she discovered they were all telling the truth.

He is a native of Hickman County. His great-grandfather was a three-term sheriff. Some of his family kept their relative, the good sheriff, busy. They liked to make and partake of what they termed the best white whiskey in the world. Except for Uncle Will. He always said he drank only for medicinal purposes.

My father and a boyhood friend knew that his Uncle Will had some whiskey hidden in the stable. Every morning they watched Uncle Will go out for a drink. Then every evening he would go back for another.

"When Uncle Will told us that he drank only for medicinal purposes, you know what we thought of that.

"We spent the better part of one summer searching the stable trying to find out where he was hiding his jug." Dad says.

"Finally, we got up in the loft and hid where we could look down and see him when he walked through the stable. Sure enough, late that evening, Uncle Will came to get his drink—for medicinal purposes only.

"Of all places, he had that gallon jug buried down in some loose wheat in a grain bin. We'd been within a foot of it a hundred times and just didn't know where to look.

"We waited until he had gone to work the next day before we headed for the stable. We got a stick and measured exactly how far the jug was from the sides of the grain bin so we could put it back in the same place. We were sure he'd never miss what little two boys would drink from his jug.

"Now, what we didn't know was that Uncle Will had put poke root in his whiskey. He was convinced that poke root helped his arthritis."

For those who don't know, poke is a weed that grows wild. When it is young, many people eat the tender leaves as "poke sallet," but as the plant matures the root takes on an awful taste, so strong and pungent that it will make castor oil welcome—and sometimes necessary.

Well, Dad hooked his finger through the handle of the jug, swung it over his shoulder, and took a pull, just as he'd seen the grownups do.

"I took a pretty good swig," he remembers. "I gagged. I couldn't speak or breathe. I thought I had been poisoned. I shoved the jug toward William and ran out of the stable, wheezing.

"The next thing I remember, William was laying on his stomach, drinking out of the pond. When he got through with his chaser, he came over to me, mad as blazes.

"'Why didn't you tell me what was in that jug?' he yelled.

"'Hell, man,' I said, 'I couldn't say a word. If I hadn't run over that hay mower, I don't believe I would have ever started breathing again.'"

Well there is always a moral to my father's stories. And that is why today, I only drink for medicinal purposes. And why I'm almost as adept at tall stories as he.

5

The Day the Jackass "Flew"

Numbers, percentages, how much, how many?

It's surprising what numbers tell us.

Harper's magazine recently published what it called some fascinating figures that are rather revealing.

For instance, do you know any people who call Mondays their favorite day of the week? I'm fortunate; I don't. But three people out of every 100 claim that.

There are 965,000 others who say they have Coca-Cola for breakfast. They don't specify, however, whether they have New Coke, Classic Coke, Diet Coke, Cherry Coke, caffeine-free, or any of the others.

Some of the numbers are frightening. Others make me mad.

It's frightening to know that 9,600 pounds of plutonium and highly enriched uranium are unaccounted for in U.S. inventories. It's more frightening to know it takes only 15 pounds of plutonium to make an atomic bomb.

It ruffles me to know that spying operations against the United States were rampant in 1985, one year after this country spent $4,327,266 on paper shredders to keep our secrets secret.

While some studies are eye-openers, some disturbing and some just interesting, others are just plain unbelievable.

I realize the whole world has changed a lot since I was in college in the late 1950s and early '60s, but it's hard to believe people have changed that much.

I read last week of a survey of 250 college students at Stanford University in California. I immediately put it in the unbelievable category.

Of the 250 students polled, according to results published in *Psychology Today*, a whopping 96 percent said they got more thrills out of a song than out of sex.

They must be listening more to Ray Stevens than they are to Dr. Ruth. I got a thrill out of Stevens' song *The Streak*, and I enjoyed his *Mississippi Squirrel*, but both were many, many thrills behind sex.

But wait, that's not all. Of those same students, 92 percent said they enjoyed a phony movie scene over a genuine steamy scene. And, 87 percent said they felt there was more beauty in nature than in being bare naked in a bedroom, preferably with someone of the opposite sex.

The guys I went to college with, I'm positive, would rather check into a hotel with Bo Derek than have a free ten-year subscription to *The Tennessee Conservationist*.

And the college women of 25 years ago? I'm just as positive they would still find more beauty in Don Johnson, Robert Redford, or even Joe Crockett Shelton than they would in an oak tree or a patch of honeysuckle.

Stanford University is an educational institution of the highest order. It has an excellent and respected reputation. But the students who participated in that survey are either too interested in their learning or they are monumental liars.

Now back to the *Harper*'s figures. They state that the longest flight recorded by a chicken is 302 feet and 8 inches. I know that one is wrong.

Because, the time my brother, Ronnie, and I hitched our jackass, Hannibal, to the coaster wagon we flushed a game settin' hen for a flight much longer than that.

Hannibal was unaccustomed to the sound of a metal wagon, so he ran away. Right after he cleared the row of hedges, he dumped us in a fence row of saw briers and sassafras bushes. He also stripped out of the harness and left the coaster wagon with us.

The ruckus of us hitting flushed the hen. As we stumbled out of the fence row kicking off briers and leaves, the hen soared out of sight behind Herschel Osborne's tobacco barn a good half mile away. Her flight path was downhill and downwind, however.

The hen never did come back. It took Hannibal three days to find his way home.

If someone had just had the foresight to record it, I'll bet Hannibal would have made the *Harper*'s list—for the longest distance covered by a scared jackass.

6

Uncle Shorty Was Confused

Most of us are familiar with the saying: "There's no free lunches anymore." Well, let me tell you about something else that's not free anymore—calendars.

I used to have more calendars than anyone could use, but no more. This year I had to buy one. Businesses once gave them away on a wholesale basis. Now it's easier to get a T-shirt or a baseball hat.

I remember as a child going to Springfield on Saturday afternoons with my grandfather. About this time of year everywhere we stopped they gave us a calendar.

Papa was never in a hurry on these trips. Often he'd take me by Qualls Motor Company and let me sit on the new John Deere tractors. Sometimes we'd go by Farmer's Supply Company, or Growers Supply. Sometimes we'd go down by Gilley Rawls' Mule Barn, or Walker Implement Company, or Craig's Restaurant, or Randolph House. My grandparents bought their groceries either at Hillie's Supermarket or City Cash Market.

Starting in December, all these places had free calendars with their names on them. And they wanted to make sure everyone had one. Since we didn't want to hurt anyone's feelings, we took a calendar from each.

It's rare to find anyone giving anything away nowadays. When I started searching for a calendar, I thought of all these places. I don't recall exactly when they stopped giving out free calendars, but they all did. Now they're all out of business. I wonder if they'd still be thriving if they'd continued to give away calendars. I don't know, but I do know it would've made my life easier. I'm lost without a calendar. I'm often lost even with one, but I feel more secure when I have one.

I was watching Charlie Chase on *Channel Four Magazine* the other day. His guest was Karen Davis of Davis-Kidd Booksellers. She'd brought with her a sampling of her store's line of calendars. She showed some calendars that cost about $12, others for about $7.50, and a leather-bound one that was obviously too expensive to mention the price publicly. Most of them had pretty pictures, beautiful landscapes, funny sayings or cartoon characters, but that's about it.

The calendars I remember getting from the now-defunct merchants were full of useful information. In addition to having the days and months in the proper order, they had many other features.

Some had symbols that forecast the weather a year in advance. They had the time of the sunrise and sunset each day, the various phases of the moon and the precise moment the changes occurred. Some had delicious recipes. Some had pouches to keep up with receipts. Others had remedies for a variety of ailments.

But almost every one of them had the signs to plant crops by. Many farmers, my grandparents included, religiously planted by the signs. They knew never to plant a crop when the sign was in the heart—the germination would be spotty and the yield would be poor without fail. However, this was an excellent sign to kill weeds. They never planted corn on the light of the moon. Corn planted at this time makes long stalks and short ears. The breast, arm and knees were some of their favorite signs.

I preferred the calendars with the weather flags. They were usually given away at grocery stores. They also advertised Cardui, for menstrual cramps and Black Draught, a strong laxative "for all the family."

I sure miss those old calendars, but I don't miss Black Draught, which is still available. It brings back unpleasant memories.

It was Uncle Shorty who discovered its versatility. My grandmother, grinning from ear to ear, told me all about it:

"Your Uncle Shorty took a double dose of Black Draught this morning. He thought he was taking cough medicine."

"Did it work?" I asked.

"Must've," she said, bursting into laughter. "See him hanging on to that fence post out by the lot? He wouldn't dare cough."

7

Sometimes Memories
Need a Little Help

Years ago we bought a trailer near here for our Shangri-La. I wish I could remember all the good times we've had there. All the great fishing trips. All the interesting people who've been there with us over the years. But I can't. Time has a way of obscuring details and names. And good times. And bad times.

Ronnie, my brother, decided to help our memory. In December 1984 he started a journal. Nothing fancy. Just a spiral notebook we leave on the counter by the sink. We write about our trips. And we ask others to make note of theirs.

"We've talked about doing this for years," Ronnie's first entry begins. "I wish we'd started it years ago. It could have recorded the happy times. The sad times. The weather, the problems, or anything else associated with our stay. . . ."

Not long ago I read it. I, too, wish we'd started it years ago. It's a good idea. I would have known exactly when the kids caught their first fish. When they first saw the beach. When we first went sailing; took the helicopter tour. And various other details that have since slipped by memory's wayside.

There's an entry in the journal from a lawyer friend who stayed there with his wife. He noted they enjoyed a lot of "golf, golf, golf, golf, eat, eat, eat, eat, and some 'censored activities.'"

21

Looking back, I remember a lot of the good times and few of the sad times. Maybe it's better that way.

However, a sad time does come to mind. It was during my single days. I took a woman down for a long weekend. I'd show off. I'd take her fishing. Cook for her. We'd dine by candlelight, and . . . .

Shortly after our midday arrival, we went fishing. She'd never caught a fish. I'm a great teacher. She caught the first fish, a nice trout. I caught the next one, a smaller saltwater catfish. Suddenly the boat lurched and the catfish stuck a bony fin deep into the side of my knee. The pain was excruciating. And it got worse.

She drove me to the hospital. The doctor removed the fin and put me on crutches. He failed to tell me the pain would get worse. I spent the next two nights sitting in a chair drinking painkiller. A sad trip, indeed.

My aunt said it was the Lord's way of delivering me from temptation.

Ronnie went down this past New Year's Day. He noted happily when he arrived that Tennessee was leading Miami in the Sugar Bowl 21–7. He said he made a fast trip noticing an "almost complete lack of police protection." His way of saying he avoided radar traps.

He also noted he had "a mild encounter with some a..hole who doesn't deserve to wear a Budweiser hat. But he did have good brakes."

I'm not going to ask about that one.

I left my own notations this trip:

"Granddaddy, [my father] Joe, Matt, and I arrived at 11 p.m. The boys had just enough sleep to be wide awake. After Granddaddy got three stations at the same time on the radio and I got two stiff drinks of gin, so was I.

"Plug dead in Granddaddy's room. No power for radio. He looked frantically for extension cord first night. Didn't find it under my bed. Next day found reason for dead plug in switchbox. Said it looked like someone killed it on purpose. Radio played all night.

"Next night radio played again all night. No one slept but Granddaddy. Can't wait to get home. I need the rest."

I also noted that Joe and Matt caught fish and crabs at the steam plant. And that our stay was extended because of the weather at home. The last entry I posted at noon Tuesday: "Hope to leave by 1 p.m. Joe and Matt want to play in snow. I want to play with Linda. And, Granddaddy wants to play his damn radio all night long."

Yep, a journal's a good idea.

PART TWO

Boyhood Memories That Last

8

The First Pocket Knife

There are few days in a young man's life that rank with the day he gets his first pocket knife.

It's a special day. A day he's waited for for years.

When I was a kid, that day usually came around your tenth birthday. However, Joe and Matt are trying to convince me the "age of first knife" has declined since I was a kid. Sounds reasonable. After all, since I got my first pocket knife, the voting age and the drinking age have come down.

Recently, my son Matt went with me to a lumber store near our home. He glued himself in front of the pocket knife display for the better part of an hour. He looked at the knives with a longing, a fondness, a wistfulness that's hard to describe. Little boys are attracted to pocket knives like metal to a magnet.

"Daddy, please, can I have that little one?"

"I don't believe you're quite ready for a knife yet."

"I'll be real careful."

"When you get older, I'll get it for you."

So far, Joe has negotiated me down to eight for his first one. And Matt is working on seven.

I remember how I felt as I fondled that little pearl-handled beauty given to me by my grandfather. I felt ten feet tall. Ronnie, my younger brother, asked to whittle with it.

"No, you're too little."

Everyone knew kids younger than ten were too irresponsible, too immature and too reckless to handle a knife.

Even I got the standard warning: "Be careful and don't cut yourself."

It seemed everyone thought that was one of the first things I would do with my new pocket knife. Unfortunately, it was.

When you get that first cut, it always looks a lot worse than it really is. There's blood everywhere. Your mother thinks her worst fears have come true. That you are cut in varying degrees all over your body.

There's blood on your jeans. On your lips (where you stuck your finger in your mouth as soon as you noticed the cut), in your hair, on your bike, on the dog, the kitchen floor, the bathroom sink, the table cloth and several other places.

You see, when you cut yourself the first time with your new pocket knife, you move around very quickly for the first few seconds, swinging your bleeding hand wildly.

But, when it's all cleaned up, the cut is usually a small one on the index finger of the hand that was holding the stick.

It's easy to convince yourself that had the knife been sharp, it would have bitten into the wood rather than your finger. So while the finger is healing you sharpen your knife. Then you test it by cutting a sheet of notebook paper. If it cuts clean you announce it's "sharp as a razor."

Usually soon after drawing first blood, the knife disappears. You're willing to bet your best beagle hound you put it in the cigar box under the bed, but it's gone the next morning.

But, if you looked broken-hearted, sad and depressed, and if you begged long enough, the knife usually turned up again in a few days. And the speech was like a television rerun:

"Be careful. Don't cut yourself."

The ultimate satisfaction of owning your first knife always came somewhat unexpectedly. And the more people standing around to witness it, the better. Especially if the onlookers were younger—still too young to have a knife of their own.

While witnessing a grown-up doing something requiring a knife, it'll happen. He'll look right at you and ask:

"You got a knife?"

You dart your hand in your pocket, withdraw your knife and open the big blade before handing it to him. And, because the grown-up asked you, you know he considers you mature and reliable enough to respect a knife. So, you tell him:

"Be careful. Don't cut yourself. It's sharp as a razor."

The other kids are filled with awe.

9

Learning to Face the Darkness

There's a time when every young man has to prove his manhood.

Sometimes he has to prove it more than once. But the toughest test is proving he's not afraid of the dark. In reality, there's no way to prove this, because everyone is afraid of the dark at some time or another. But there are ways to develop raw courage to disguise your fear.

The methods vary widely. For a country boy it's especially difficult. There're no street lights in the country.

Sleeping out in the yard usually comes first. Initial attempts are usually with someone who has done it previously. Still, it may take several tries before staying out long enough to hear a rooster crow or see a sunrise.

Yard sleeping is just a prelude to the real test. The real test comes when a country boy is old enough, and brave enough, to attempt a night on the creek bank.

Most creek banks are very dark. Trees overhang the water and block out all light. Strange sounds permeate the darkness. The fire seems dim and constantly on the verge of dying out altogether.

Spending the night on a creek bank is not something a boy

does without proper preparation. First, you've got to learn to whistle. I don't know why it is, but when you're out after dark it always helps to whistle.

Others can help, too. An older brother, for instance, can be a tremendous asset in toughening you up for a dark night outside. He can jump out from behind bushes, the garage, the stable, or most anywhere else as long as he does it totally unexpectedly. You'd be surprised how tough this makes a younger brother.

Or he can see his little brother coming toward the house after dark and run and turn off all the porch lights and any others that might even partially illuminate his way. This helps develop speed.

Unfortunately, I never had an older brother to help prepare me for such adventures in the darkness. But the fact that I was deprived didn't keep me from helping my brother Ronnie.

More than once, he has tossed a bucket of fresh, warm milk high into the air, screamed piercingly, and ran for home faster than a minnow can swim a dipper. Usually, it was because I had jumped from behind bushes, the garage, the stable, or most anywhere else, as he came home from milking the cow. He still doesn't fully appreciate the advantage a younger brother has in darkness preparation.

Once, he was at my grandmother's house long after dark. Mother sent me to accompany him home. I had a flashlight, and he didn't. Just before I got to the house, the back door opened. I saw Ronnie walking across the cistern porch. Old Duke, his bulldog and constant companion, was lying out in the yard waiting for Ronnie.

A dog is also a great help in the dark. That is, except when the dog sees something you can't, yelps like he's been shot, and makes a beeline for home without you. Those occasions can be especially unnerving.

As Ronnie came off the porch, I felt it an excellent time to continue his preparation. I hid behind the box elder tree. This time, I didn't jump out. I didn't yell. I just reached out and clamped my hands tight around his leg when he passed.

For just a moment, there was total silence. He didn't move

for approximately three-sixteenths of a split second. Then he ripped free amidst a chorus of screams and yells I haven't heard since. After briefly running in place, like a drag racer spinning its wheels, he finally got traction.

He was like a streak, screaming through the yard. Then he collided with Old Duke. The sound of the collision chilled my blood. There was growling and screaming. And there were bites and scratches over most of his body, his legs, his stomach, his hips.

After tender care, a lot of medicine, and a lot of patience, Old Duke finally recovered, and Ronnie was ready to face the darkness.

10

Hot Tubs, Quiche, and Ceiling Fans

Some country boys feel out of place in today's world of white wine, hot tubs, ceiling fans, gas lights and quiche.

Take hot tubs for instance. I've seen a few of these things and even used a few. They are usually made of fiberglass or redwood and have pumps to keep the warm water circulating. Most of them are big enough for several people, but when I hop into one, I usually displace more than my share of water.

They are highly advertised, touted by those who use them, and longed for by those who don't have them. They also cost about two thousand dollars.

I've never been too excited by them, however. I guess it's because I enjoyed hot tubs 40 years ago, long before they became the "in" thing for Yuppies. In fact, my brother and I had the pleasure of hot tubs a couple of times a week and always on Saturday.

Ours was basically the same as those today. It just didn't have all the amenities.

Ours was made of galvanized metal. The water was heated in the summer by setting the tub in the sun in the morning. And in the winter it was heated on the kitchen stove.

Not only did Ronnie and I cleanse our bodies in our hot tub, it was fun.

So when I see the ads that show couples sitting in a tub of warm, bubbling water, laughing and sipping white wine, I know they are having fun. But if they had a bar of soap, they'd have more bubbles. Us old time hot tubbers know that the more bubbles, the more fun. I speak from experience.

Then take ceiling fans. It may seem silly to some people to sit in an air conditioned room with a ceiling fan going. It's not silly to me, it's nostalgia.

A fan moves air. That's what it is designed to do. That's what it does. It makes no difference whether it's made from palm leaves and swished back and forth, whether it's made from cardboard with a picture of Jesus on the front and the name of a funeral home on the back, or whether it's got spinning blades and hangs from the ceiling.

The ceiling fans of today are not unlike the ones I, as a boy, sat under in the soda fountain at the drug store on Main Street. Or the ones that spun so lazily in the department store or the Midway Cafe. Like present-day hot tubs, they just have more amenities.

They have reversible motors so that if you get tired of them blowing you can cause them to suck. They've got lights just like the ones we had in the schoolroom, and they've got a rheostat that varies the speed of the motor from somewhere between a gentle breeze to something akin to a mild hurricane.

Take quiche. Please take quiche. Recently, there was a popular book titled *Real Men Don't Eat Quiche*. That wasn't always the case though. I remember big, burly, farmhands gobbling up my grandmother's cheese pie. They were real men. Darned if I can tell the difference in my grandmother's cheese pie and the quiche you get in restaurants today, except my grandmother's was better.

Take gas lights. People today think they are classy, stylish, uptown. They have them on antique-looking posts out at the end of the driveway.

We had a gas light in the house. It was essential. Out in the country where we lived, the power was frequently disrupted. Many times I've done my homework by that old gas light.

Ronnie and I didn't realize how lucky we were. Little did we know we were living 40 years before our time. We never tried to take a bath with one hand while holding a glass of white wine in the other.

But any of you good ole boys who feel out of place with hot tubs, quiche, gas lights and ceiling fans, don't. My grandmother used to say "everything that goes around, comes around."

We've just come around.

11

A Hair-Curling Yarn

My grandmother tried every folk remedy she heard of to make my hair curly.

First, when I was a baby, she washed my hair in pure sour-mash whiskey. I don't know where she heard this would make my hair curly, but I'm sure it had some validity.

I think, though, she probably got the directions a little mixed up. I learned in later years that pure sour-mash whiskey will indeed curl your hair. But, only when it's taken internally.

As I grew older, my grandmother abandoned the whiskey shampoos and turned to food as curling agents. First it was carrots. Raw carrots, she said, would curl my locks. Then it was a variety of other foods. And finally she capped the list of curl-producing foods with gizzards from chickens and turkeys.

I don't remember being especially fond of the vegetables, but I kind of liked the whiskey and the gizzards.

Once I was watching her clean a nice, plump baking hen. After scalding it in the wash kettle of steaming hot water, she carefully plucked off the feathers. Then she was ready to split it open.

I asked a string of questions about each part as she removed it. Some, she threw into the bucket with the wet feathers, and others she put into a pan of clean water.

That's the first time I ever saw a chicken's craw. I watched her cut it open and clean it out. It was full of small rocks and sand. I was fascinated. I fully expected her to toss it into the feather bucket after she showed me its contents. Instead she tossed it into the pan of clean water. Right in with the liver and the wings.

"You're not going to save that thing, are you?" I asked.

"Sure I am," she said. "That's one of your favorite parts. It's the gizzard. It'll make your hair curly."

I had eaten gizzards. I liked gizzards. But that was before I knew they were just a sack of rocks. I never was that fond of curly hair, and suddenly I lost my fondness for gizzards.

In time I regained my taste for gizzards, but I never again witnessed one being cleaned.

I don't know what it was. It could have been the whiskey. It could have been the variety of vegetables. It could have been the gizzards. It could have been any number of other things, but when I was a child, I had curly hair. And my grandmother took credit for it.

My curly locks remained until I started losing my hair just after leaving high school. I joked with my grandmother that it was probably because of the whiskey She surprised me and agreed.

"Oh, it's whiskey all right," she said. "You'd still have hair and you'd still have curls if you'd continued to wash your hair in it instead of drinking it. It caused your hair to fall out, and it caused mine and your mother's to turn gray."

A recent short wire story out of Kansas City brought all this to mind.

A grocery store owner and his butcher were fined a total of four thousand dollars for misbranding meat as "fresh ground beef" and "pork sausage" that was actually forty percent ground turkey gizzards.

The defendants bought 76,600 pounds of turkey gizzards in

just over a year to mix with meat, according to invoices gathered by the U.S. Department of Agriculture. The store was able to increase its profits by almost fifty-five thousand dollars by mixing turkey gizzards with beef and pork, prosecutors said.

The late Junior Samples told a story that bore a striking resemblance. He said he heard of a restaurant operator caught putting horse meat into his chicken salad. When asked the percentage, he said, "Half and half, one horse and one chicken."

I'm glad the fellows in Kansas City were brought to justice.

They made fifty-five thousand dollars in profits by mixing in the gizzards. Then they were fined four thousand dollars. That leaves a net profit of fifty-one thousand dollars.

If that kind of justice doesn't curl your hair, neither will a whiskey shampoo.

12

Return to Sycamore Creek

There are few things about childhood that evoke more pleasant memories than trips to the Old Swimming Hole on Sycamore Creek.

Some things never seem to change and the Old Swimming Hole is one of them.

The other day, I took Joe and Matt to a spot where I used to swim. Some of my fondest memories are of my dad and me splashing in that same cool, clear water. The creek is wide and shallow. And it still smells fresh. There always seems to be a cool breeze.

We waded in the shallow water and gently lifted rocks and caught crayfish. We waded. We splashed. We laughed. And we had it all to ourselves.

Joe wanted to fish. He kept shooing Matt and me away from his fishing spot.

We waded downstream and found a deep hole that was over Matt's head. But he loved it. It gave him a chance to show off what he had learned after two weeks of swimming lessons at the East Nashville YMCA.

There were no concrete steps, no slick tile, no underwater

lights, no deck chairs; and no one had checked the purity of the water.

There was just a gradual sloping bank on one side, a gravel bar on the other and squishy mud and wet leaves underfoot. Out in the middle, the strong current has swept the bottom clean and there is nothing but smooth, solid rock.

Matt jumped as far as he could out toward the middle, made a big splash and went under.

When he surfaced, he shook his head, grabbed a quick breath and started swimming toward me. His form was pretty good: a passable flutter kick, a decent crawl stroke, face in the water. His head came up for a quick breath. Another kick, stroke and breath and he touched me. I was proud of him.

His face, now barely above the water as he stood tiptoe, beamed with pride.

"Now, Dad," he said with the seriousness of a four-year-old going on 60, "that was heavy duty."

Joe, giving up on the fish, joined us.

"Did you swim here when you were a little boy?" he asked.

"I sure did."

"Did Granddaddy bring you?"

"He did when I was little. He loved to swim. He taught me how to swim and float on my back."

I continued to reminisce.

Later, when we were a little older, my brother Ronnie and I rode our bikes here.

There is a spot a little farther downstream, now fenced off, where older boys hung a steel cable high in a sycamore tree.

You climbed up the bank, took the end of the cable, and held tight. When you left the bank, there was no turning back. You sailed out over the water in a wide, swinging arc, then dropped into the deep hole.

One day we dared our cousin, Rex, a city boy who had done his swimming only in pools with diving boards and lifeguards, to try the swing. He climbed up the bank and, after a long, doubtful pause, pushed off.

Wide and high he went, out over the hole. But he froze. He wouldn't turn loose.

He sailed back toward the steep mud bank, his speed increasing. When he hit the side of the bank, it sounded like a bullfrog being swatted with a canoe paddle. Splat! Whoosh! It knocked all the air out of his body.

We dragged him up to a grassy spot and finally got him breathing again. Rural life lost its charm that day for Rex.

The cable is gone now. But the surrounding area is much the same. Lush, rolling farmland and pastures.

Earlier in the day, our church had a baptism here. That hasn't changed either.

I wish the area could stay the same, that Matt and Joe could bring their sons here and tell them about our first visit. I wish that four decades hence they still would hold Sunday afternoon baptisms right here in this pretty spot.

I wish it. But I know better. I know that "progress" is coming. And even the work of the Lord will have to give way to progress.

13

Cowboy Dreams

I was just finishing my second year of college when Dad came up to my bedroom one Saturday morning for a serious talk.

Dad rarely initiated serious discussions. This day was an exception.

"Son," he began, "you've had a couple of jobs, and now you're finishing another year of college. I think it's about time to decide what you want to do with your life. Your mother and I are concerned you haven't decided what you want to do."

"I've given this a lot of thought," I said. I noticed a smile crossing dad's face. "After serious consideration and weighing all the pros and cons of what the world has to offer, I've reached a decision. I want to be a cowboy."

Dad wasn't smiling anymore. I could tell by his look that my future, if I had one, was in jeopardy. Fortunately, he regained control before resorting to violence.

Sometimes I still want to be a cowboy. I can't think of any farm boy who grew up in the 1950s who didn't, at one time or another, want to be a cowboy.

It coincided with the spread of television sets to rural areas. Every afternoon, we watched cowboy movies on television. Hours and hours of Hoot Gibson, Hopalong Cassidy, Roy

Rogers and Dale Evans, Gene Autry, Tex Ritter, The Cisco Kid, and many more.

My brother Ronnie and I once saw a short segment of a rodeo in one of the cowboy movies. At the time, we had a young Jersey bull about two months old. We started training the calf to be a rodeo bull and we trained as clowns. We used a tow sack to wave in the calf's face. He didn't like it right off. That suited us fine. He had spirit.

A few days later, we had him charging the sack Then he was charging us. We got some real good clown training because it usually took one of us to distract him while the other one got to the fence.

We did all this training without our grandfather's knowledge, of course. But Papa noticed the bull had "a kinda mean disposition" when he took him to pasture at the Old Place—37 acres of rocks and hills about a mile from where we lived.

The newness of his surroundings kept the young bull, which weighed several hundred pounds by this time, occupied for the first few days. But within a week, he caught Papa coming up the hill from the creek. The bull, in true rodeo fashion, pawed his feet in the dirt, snorted a few times, then charged.

Papa knew he'd never make the fence. So, he climbed the old pear tree, the only tree in the field. Papa made it to the lower branches before the bull slammed his head into the tree trunk. For the next two hours, Papa was treed by the bull. Papa picked the young, hard, green pears and threw them down at the bull, but it just seemed to make him madder. The bull, that is. Papa couldn't get any madder.

Finally, the bull tired and ambled off toward the creek. Papa scampered for the fence and came home to a cold lunch, but he was still hot enough to make up for it.

The next day, the bull went to market. Papa wasn't mad any more. And Ronnie and I never again trained any rodeo stock. But I still dream of being a cowboy.

PART THREE

Husband and Father

14

"Can We Talk?"

When Joan Rivers smiles and asks, "Can we talk?" I laugh.
When a 6-year-old boy named Joe, unsmiling, asks, "Can we talk?" I don't laugh.

It happened just yesterday. Joe was serious. He had just the hint of a frown on his face.

"Sure we can talk, Joe," I said.

"Well," he said, "Charlie told me that somebody was going to shoot Santa Claus. Is that right?"

"No, Joe. Everyone loves Santa. No one will ever shoot him."

"Are you sure?"

"Sure, I'm sure."

"Then why did Charlie tell me that?"

"Now I'm not sure about that. But for some reason older boys sometimes tell little boys things to make them worry. Maybe some big boys told them things like that when they were little."

Had the frown vanished?

"Santa will be all right, Joe. Just wait and see. It's only four more days before the big day."

He reminded me that he and Matt, who is four, have been on their best conduct.

"The days really seem long when you're being good, don't they?"

"Yeah."

A week ago we had visited a department store Santa.

Oh, for the faith of a little boy! The fake white beard, so transparent to an adult, was invisible to Joe as he poured out his fishing tackle wish list.

Santa looked to me like a fellow who wouldn't know a trout from a salmon without a French menu. He couldn't hide his puzzlement as Joe said, "I want a Mud Bug, an ABU Reflex and a Rooster Tail Spinner. I want the Rooster Tail to tie behind the Mud Bug. And I want a Zebco 33 and an open face."

Joe was probably the only kid there who didn't go for the current fad and ask for a talking bear.

I was proud of my lad.

That was a week ago. Now, looking into his trusting face, I saw the hint of the frown again.

"Daddy, there's something else."

"What's that, Joe?"

"Do big boys always make things up about Santa Claus?"

"I'm sure they don't do it always. Why?"

Now I'm asking him questions.

"Well, another boy at school said there wasn't any Santa Claus."

"What did you say to that?"

"I told him there was, too."

"So?"

"Well, I've been thinking and wondering. I remember that last year when we got presents from Santa, we also got presents from you and mom."

"Of course you did."

"Well, Santa's presents were wrapped in the same kind of paper as the presents from you and mom."

"Maybe Santa got his paper at Wal-Mart too."

"C'mon, dad, is there really a Santa Claus?"

Oh, for the faith of a little boy.

He has so much time to learn about fraud, deceit, misrepresentation. And so soon he must lose that childlike faith. How to answer?

"Joe, do you know who Santa Claus really is?"

"Who?"

"He is the real spirit of Christmas, Joe. And that spirit is as real as you and me. Think about that first Christmas, Joe. The spirit of giving started that night. The world was given a new baby, Jesus. The three Wise Men brought gifts to the new baby. That's where the spirit of Christmas began. Santa carries on that spirit. Santa teaches us that the true spirit of Christmas is in giving, whatever the wrapping on the package.

"And when little boys believe in Santa, they carry on that same spirit. So as long as you believe in the Christmas spirit, you will also believe in Santa Claus."

Now the frown is gone. The smile is a big one.

"You know something, Dad, I'm always gonna believe in Santa Claus."

"Me, too, son. Me, too."

15

On Being a Pal

As parents know, young children require almost constant supervision. There was a time, however, when this supervision fell mainly on the shoulders of mothers.

Fortunately, times have changed. While some fathers cling to the old-fashioned way, others welcome the chance to spend more time with their children.

I remember about 15 years ago when I would take Todd to the doctor's office I would be the only male there—except for the doctor. Now when I take Joe and Matt, there are as many fathers there with children as there are mothers. And the doctor is just as likely to be a woman as a man.

The cigarette ads that proclaim, "You've come a long way, baby," are aimed at highlighting the progress made by women. I see fathers as having come a long way, too.

I enjoy being with my boys. I'm sorry I didn't have more time to spend with Todd when he was young.

Recently Linda was off work and had several errands to do. I decided to give the baby sitter a day off too, so I planned my day to include Joe and Matt.

Shortly after Linda left, we discussed making a rabbit box to see if we could catch a wild rabbit.

"What would you fellows do if you went out to check the box and found a rabbit?" I asked.

"I'd raise the door and wait for him to get out," Joe said. "I wouldn't want to hurt him."

"Yeah, That's what we'd do. We'd turn him loose," Matt agreed.

"Sometimes other animals get caught in a rabbit box," I told them. "What would you do if you checked the box and found a skunk?"

"I'd come and get you," Joe said, "and tell you I didn't know what it was."

I was amused at their demonic laugh as they thought about that prospect.

"Daddy, Daddy," Matt said urgently. "What if we find a great, great, big 'nake in there? You know what I would do?"

"No, tell me what you would do."

"I wouldn't open the door."

We finally decided we didn't really want to catch a rabbit anyway, so the rabbit box never got past the discussion stage. Instead we hauled some wood and then went fishing. Within minutes Joe had hooked a pound-sized bream. Then Matt caught one. There was lots of laughter, giggles, big brags, and excitement galore.

I was suddenly busier than a one-armed wallpaper hanger with a bad case of poison ivy. I was baiting hooks, taking off fish, and retrieving lines from nearby trees.

Then the bass started hitting. Joe had caught his first bass at this pond, so he knew immediately what he had hooked when the two-pounder broke water and walked on his tail.

While Joe and I were admiring the bass, Matt moved his bait to the exact spot Joe was fishing when he hooked the bass. I spent the next few minutes refereeing. The break was welcome.

After we had caught enough for supper that night, I convinced the boys we should leave and have the fish fried by the time Linda got home. First, we made a quick run to the grocery.

It was at the grocery store that I ran into an old schoolmate I hadn't seen in years. He has three children, all of them much older than Joe and Matt. I remember, when we were in closer contact, that he had little to do with his children until they were old enough to help out in the fields. When they were younger, they were his wife's responsibility. It's unfortunate he still doesn't know what he missed.

After some small talk, and upon hearing Joe and Matt tell about the fishing trip, he said, "You must've lost the toss."

"What do you mean?"

"I figured you and Linda tossed a coin to see who would keep the boys, and you lost."

"Nope, I won."

16

Pumpkin Pleasures

Charlie Brown usually spends several days of his comic strip anticipating the arrival of the Great Pumpkin each Halloween.

To Charlie Brown the Great Pumpkin is real.

To our family, it was real this year, too.

Early last spring when the days started getting warm and the grass green, we noticed a mystery plant near the front porch. As the leaves grew larger the plant developed runners.

"Maybe it's a pumpkin," Linda said one morning as we all gathered around to check its progress. "That's near where we carved the jack-o'-lantern last Halloween."

"Yep, a punkin. That's what it is," said Joe, with all the confidence of a horticulturist. "I remember throwing the seeds right there."

The final determination, however, was still weeks away because the plant bloomed bright orange blooms each morning only to have them wilt and fall off by nightfall. Then one night I noticed a bloom that still looked healthy. The next morning, an inspection confirmed Joe was right. There was a small "punkin" just beginning to develop at the base of the bloom.

"That's gonna be my punkin," Joe announced.

"No, it's my punkin," Matt said. "Daddy, tell Joe it's my punkin. I saw it first."

That first conflict over our Great Pumpkin was just the beginning.

I had grown pumpkins before, My grandfather and I would plant them in the corn after we had "laid it by" with the last plowing. I'll always remember the excitement of finding the pumpkins as we gathered the corn in early October. However, I don't remember ever seeing the plants as they grew and as the pumpkins developed.

I didn't know what I was missing.

As our "punkin" plant grew throughout the summer, there was rarely a day everyone in the family didn't check its progress.

It finally bore three pumpkins. Two about the same size, and a smaller one the boys quickly decided should belong to Linda.

The vine was vigorous. It grew all along the front of the porch and occasionally into the driveway. When this happened, we carefully trained it back alongside the porch.

But there were days when the pumpkin got less than loving attention, too.

"Daddy," Matt said, almost in tears as he met me at carside one afternoon, "Joe scratched my punkin. Can I scratch his?"

"I did not, Daddy," Joe yelled as he ran toward us. "Spanky [our beagle] did it. And Matt saw him do it, too."

"Did not."

"Did too."

"Let me take a look," I suggested.

As we inspected the pumpkin, I was amazed at the dexterity of ole Spanky. He carved an almost perfect "J" on Matt's pumpkin and even left the nail beside it.

There was another big day when everyone had to come look, the day Joe noticed the first tinge of orange on his pumpkin. Soon Matt's turned orange too.

Then Halloween arrived. This year, the jack-o'-lanterns had special meaning. We knew their heritage. We had seen them grow from small green balls to giant orange globes.

The freeze got the last remnants of the vine. I miss seeing it when I get home at night. And I miss seeing the spontaneous excitement of the boys as they watched and marveled at the day-to-day changes from the emergence of the mysterious plant to the laughs and giggles generated by the ugly jack-o'-lanterns.

The miracle of its growth taught us that some of life's great pleasures are accidental; some really significant experiences—the kind that leave lasting memories—are rarely planned.

Thank you, Great Pumpkin, for those lessons and the pleasure you gave us.

We know how you feel, Charlie Brown.

17 _____

Dad Doesn't Always
Know Best

How easily we forget that the world of children is so
different from our adult world. We look into their faces and
sometimes their innocence lets us ignore how fragile is their
understanding of us.

Our son Joe just finished his first year of school. It ended on a
high for him, but because of my failure to understand that
fragility, it didn't begin that way.

I remember that first day nine months ago. Every hair was in
place, his new clothes crisply pressed, but his small chin
trembled as he spoke. I knew he was scared, but I knew it would
be all right. I remembered my own first day jitters. It would
pass.

Linda said, "Joe is nervous about going to school."

I nodded sagely, "Of course. So was I. Boys will be boys."

I should have said, "Fathers will be fathers."

The ride to school was silent. Joe was pensive. Obviously he
was thinking of this new universe he was entering: kids he
didn't know, names he didn't know, a teacher he had never seen.
They all would view him with a skeptical eye. Sure. I knew how
it was.

At school, his hand clutched mine as I walked him to his classroom; and when I left, he gazed plaintively at me as if to ask whether I really was going to leave him. I thought I saw a tear forming, and I turned away so he couldn't see my eyes mist over. I was remembering my own first day. And I was thinking, "Hang in there, Joe. It's new, but you're going to love it."

Joe was haunted by ghosts I had never known. And, without knowing it, I had helped create these ghosts.

In the weeks as he prepared for the coming experience at school, I had been getting him ready to go out into the big, bad world. Like many other parents, I wanted to warn my son about dangers that concern us all.

I had warned him about kidnappers. I had explained about the dangers of getting into cars with people he didn't know. I had cautioned about speaking to strangers on the street. I had warned him about adults who prey on children. I had explained all the fears that parents have these days when they think of their children alone, away from home.

I had told him about it again and again and again.

Joe had seen all the television shows and heard all the commercials. Older kids told stories that only reinforced his fears. He had heard more than he needed to about kidnappings and child abuse.

And so that first day, and each day thereafter, was a new fright for him. Each day he went off to school expecting the worst. And each day I convinced myself that things were getting better for him, that the jitters were wearing off. They weren't.

Linda got to the heart of it while I was on an out-of-town assignment. She was going to take him to school that morning, but she could hardly get him out of the house. He finally spent the day at the sitter's with his younger brother, Matt.

That night, Linda probed beneath the surface of his fears, and it all came pouring out. Fortunately, Linda was able, through thoughtful and sensitive explanations, to chase away the ghosts. She put those warnings I had expressed to Joe in context. She reassured him. She began reinforcing a foundation of self-confidence that I had shaken. The fears began to recede.

Next day Joe went off to school feeling better about himself and about school.

When Linda told me, I felt terrible. When Joe came home that night, I was there to talk to him about it.

In the days and weeks that followed, Joe met new people, made new friends, learned how to read, to write, to count. His teacher, Miss Swann, introduced him to the wonder of using his mind and the joy of achieving. She taught him lessons about learning and lessons about life.

And along the way, I learned the most important lesson. It's this: Fathers shouldn't think they know it all. They don't.

18

A Child's Compassion

Matthew, who had just turned four years old, and I were in the living room getting ready to start our day, his at the baby sitter's and mine at the office. Suddenly, a sharp, ear-splitting "crack" like a gunshot startled us both. We jumped and ducked.

"What was that?" Matt asked.

I looked to the window, expecting to find shattered glass. All I saw was a trickle of blood marring the clear pane.

We went to the window and looked out. A large, beautiful cardinal, lying by the rosebush, didn't move.

Matt and I went outside. I picked up the lifeless bird. Its neck was broken. Blood smeared its beak.

My mind went back to a snowy January day. Perched on the bare limbs of our peach tree were three cardinals. They shivered from the bitter cold.

We—Joe, Matt and I—decided there would be no better time to build a bird feeder.

Off to the basement we went. With a plastic milk jug, an old pie pan, and a piece of tin I fashioned a crude bird feeder and attached it to the house so we could view it from the kitchen.

Joe and Matt spent that afternoon watching the feeder,

waiting for the first bird to arrive. Darkness brought no birds, but a couple of disappointed boys.

Early the next morning Joe woke me.

"Come look out the window," he whispered with an enthusiasm that comes early only to an excited five-year-old. "A big bunch are out there. And two of them are the red birds that were cold yesterday."

The happy insistence of childhood discovery can be a magnet, even to a feeder maker who had stayed up too late. Downstairs, Matt joined us, rubbing sleep from his eyes. We peeked through the window and there they were: Joe's "big bunch of birds," two of them red. The bird feeder worked.

I enjoyed the sight as much as the boys. For most of that day we watched the birds come and go.

As the months passed, we kept the feeder filled to welcome many different kinds of birds. Of all the feathered visitors, our favorites were the cardinals.

Now Matt, who had heard talk of death, was experiencing it for the first time.

"What happened to him?" he asked.

"He saw the sky reflected in the window," I said. "It was like looking into a mirror. He just flew into it and died."

I placed the bird on the ground near the rosebush. As I turned away, Matt picked it up and cradled the cardinal in his tiny hands.

"We have to leave the bird, son. I have to get to work."

"No," he said with a drill sergeant's authority. But who ever saw a drill sergeant with a tear trickling down his cheek?

"I've seen the cat chase the birds," he said. "If we leave him here the cat will get him. He's my friend and I'm going to take him with me."

Work would just have to wait. How can you force a child to desert a lost friend? How could you ignore human compassion born so early in a young boy's breast?

I explained that we couldn't take the bird with us, that when there is death, the proper thing is a funeral. Matt listened and nodded understanding and acceptance.

And so we conducted a brief funeral and simple burial. Matt cried. Watching him weep, I felt a tear on my cheek. We both felt better when it was over.

Matt was quiet as we drove to the sitter's. Just before we arrived, he asked: "Daddy, do birds go to Heaven?"

"I hope so, Matt. I really hope so."

19

The Tooth Fairy

To young children, losing baby teeth is a fact of life.

For some it's a traumatic experience. A tooth comes out, and there is a gaping hole. There's blood. And usually tears. But some kids don't seem to mind losing teeth; they know they will be rewarded by the Tooth Fairy.

Our son Joe falls in this last category. He recently lost two baby teeth after having worked diligently to loosen them.

You see, Joe is on another one of his savings kicks. And when he's in this mode, he amasses money until he gets enough to buy whatever he's saving for. This time, it's an open-faced fishing reel and rod.

Between these periods of frugality, money means nothing. He can walk right by a dime on the floor without picking it up and hoarding it away. He can watch television without checking under the cushions of the couch and chairs. He can ride in the car without removing the back seat to check for loose coins.

When he came to me wanting his tooth out, he was enthusiastic.

"Dad, I've been working on it all day," he said. "Just feel how loose it is."

"Maybe we'd better give it another day or two," I said, after finding it still pretty snug.

"Aw, c'mon, Dad. It's ready. Here's the string."

I took the dental floss and made a slip knot, the same kind my grandfather used when he pulled my baby teeth. Then I slipped it around his tooth. Finally, we were ready.

I supported his head against my body and prepared for a quick jerk on the string. I jerked. The string broke. The tooth was bleeding, but still firmly implanted.

"See, Joe," I said. "I don't think it's quite ready."

"Yes it is, too. The string's just not strong enough. It'll come out this time."

I doubled the floss and put it back on the tooth. A quick jerk again. The string held. The tooth was out. Joe was ecstatic.

Later, I said to Linda that Joe was the toughest little boy I'd ever seen. I was proud of the courage he showed by standing there, not once but twice, as I jerked out his tooth.

"He's not all that tough," she said. "He's mercenary."

Joe went to sleep that night in my bed as Linda read him and Matt a story. After they drifted off, she tucked them away in their own beds.

About 3:30 a.m., I was awakened by something moving back and forth under my pillow. It was Joe's hand.

"What are you doing?" I asked.

"I'm looking for my dollar."

"Your what?"

"My dollar the Tooth Fairy left."

"How do you know she left a dollar?" I can refer to the Tooth Fairy as "she" because I know her personally.

"I checked at school. That's what everybody gets."

"At least he knows the going rate," Linda said, obviously annoyed at our pre-dawn conversation. "Check under your own pillow, Joe."

The next night, Joe was back with another piece of string and another loose tooth. I didn't argue. I jerked.

This time the tooth not only separated from his mouth, it also separated from the string and sailed across the kitchen.

Joe was on the errant tooth like the proverbial duck on a June bug. He barely stifled a mild profanity as he leaped toward where it landed.

"Joe, it's just a tooth. Don't get upset."

"Just a tooth, my foot. It's worth a dollar."

"See, I told you he was mercenary," Linda said. "I'm gonna lock my purse in the trunk of the car."

And I'm gonna try to get Joe busy on the federal deficit. If President Reagan shared Joe's intensity, the deficit would be eliminated before Joe wets a fishing line.

The Tooth Fairy would sure be busy, though.

20

The Wonder and Pain of Love

Most of us remember falling in love as a wonderful experience. Time has a way of obscuring the unpleasant aspects, if there were any.

For others, however, falling in love can be painful. Especially if it's the first time. I saw how painful it can get just a few days ago. And it brought back many old memories.

I remember how my knees would sometimes get weak when I saw certain little girls in school. If they'd only known how madly in love I was with them, it would probably have been wonderful. But since I was too bashful to tell them, I only remember the pain.

If I saw an object of my undying love walking hand in hand with another boy, it was devastating. I'd get depressed. I'd become accident prone. I'd lose my appetite. And I'd fantasize that he'd fall through the floor of the outhouse while I swept my true love off to some tropical paradise to live happily ever after. Fantasies rarely pan out.

Matt, our five-year-old, is madly in love. He's barely into his first year of kindergarten, and already he has all the symptoms. He bathes several times a day. He uses generous amounts of my shaving lotion. He keeps his hair combed. He sometimes gazes off into space, even when dinner is on the table. And he recently had to have stitches twice in a three-day period.

We were shopping a few days ago when he saw a ring he wanted for his girlfriend. "Hey dad, can we buy Lindy this ring?" he asked. "She'd just love it. She loves rings."

I checked the price. A mere $429. Needless to say, Matt and Lindy didn't get engaged that night. However, he's pulled every wildflower he could find and even stalked Linda's rose bushes for late blossoms to keep Lindy happy.

I met Lindy a few days ago. She's in kindergarten, too. When school started she started staying after school with the same sitter who keeps Joe and Matt. Lindy is a heart stopper. With long locks of naturally curly hair and a disarming smile, she's beautiful. Matt has good taste.

When I stopped to pick up the boys, Matt and Lindy were holding hands. She had on a heavy load of makeup, complete with eye shadow. She apparently accomplished her makeover without the sitter's knowledge. Matt had every hair in place.

"Do I have to go home now?" Matt asked pleadingly. "Lindy's still here. Can't you come back later?"

Joe was already in the car, urging Matt to get in also. Lindy came to my window, and we talked.

"I may go see my boyfriend tonight," she said. I noticed Matt was suddenly very quiet.

"Do you have a boyfriend?" I asked.

"I've got two," she said.

Matt perked up a little. Then she named them. One was Chris, and the other one I can't recall. The significant thing, his name was not Matt.

It was back to depression city for Matt. His face was as long as a bad dream. Joe pressed the issue:

"What about Matt? He's your boyfriend too."

"No, he's not," she said, moving closer to my window as if she wanted to have a confidential discussion.

"One of them is my boyfriend," she said in almost a whisper, "but it's Joe."

The confidentiality didn't last long. She blurted out that Joe was her choice. All the way home Matt didn't have much to say. He didn't come when he was called to supper. He was still rather quiet as if in deep thought. Finally, he brightened up.

"Joe," he said, "I'll let you play with my water gun if you'll let me be Lindy's boyfriend."

"Sure," Joe said without hesitation. Then everything was back to normal.

I'd kinda like to be around when they break the news to Lindy. As I said, falling in love can sometimes be painful.

I just hope neither of them requires more stitches.

21 _____

A Fan in the Stands

A ball park is a world unto itself.

The noise, the hustle-bustle activity, the smell of hot dogs, and the taste of a cold beer—these are the things that make baseball the nation's favorite pastime.

And there is a special appeal at a so-called "minor league park." You won't find any $250,000-a-year strikers in Nashville or Asheville, Birmingham or Buffalo.

I had forgotten how much fun a ball game can be. But this week Linda and I took Joe and Matt to the Sounds game.

It was the night The Famous Chicken came to town. More than 14,000 turned out to see the Chicken—and some to see the game with Louisville, too.

A baseball fan is special. He or she must be patient, calm, understanding and not too thirsty.

A fan who takes a couple of little boys to their first game also must be a walking encyclopedia.

The questions started in the car, when stadium traffic came to a standstill.

"Are we gonna park here, Daddy?"

"No, Son. It's just that everyone is going to the game and it takes time to get into the parking lots."

"Is the Chicken already there?"

"I'm sure he is."

"Where did he park?"

The seats just on the first base side of home plate were excellent. The players were warming up.

"When are they going to play, Daddy?"

"They'll start in a few minutes."

"Where's the Chicken?"

"I don't know."

"I'm thirsty."

"Me too."

Linda volunteered to get Cokes and hot dogs. I volunteered to go for the beer.

When she got back, the game was in the first inning. The questions were in the bottom of the sixth.

"How many outs do they get before they go out in the field?"

"Three."

"Where's the Chicken?"

"I don't know."

"Can I see a grand slam?"

I had been looking for the beer man again. I looked the field over.

"Okay, here's your chance to see a grand slam. The bases are loaded."

The fellow in front turned around and gave me this funny look. Then the guy on third base calmly walked back to the coach's box.

"Sorry about that, Joe. This won't be your chance to see a grand slam."

"Where's the Chicken?" Matt asked.

"I think he must be with the beer man."

Finally, a roar went up from the crowd. Way out in left field we spotted the Chicken. He ran to the home plate area, turning flips, shaking his tail, waving to the spectators.

The crowd loved the Chicken. Matt squealed with delight.

During play, the Chicken led cheers atop the dugouts.

Between innings, he pretended to collide with the catcher and exchanged tosses with the players.

At one point, he took a baby from the stands for a photo. As he escorted the babe back to its parents he enclosed the child's head in his large beak. The crowd laughed. So did the baby.

As he continued his antics the boys continued the questions.

"Daddy, what is a called strike?"

"It is one you can blame on the umpire."

"Why is that player walking to the base and all the others have to run?"

"He got four balls."

"He has?"

"No! He did."

The man in front looked around again.

The Chicken was going from one dugout to the other, accompanied by two state troopers as security guards.

"Why did they arrest the Chicken, Daddy?"

"He tripped the beer man. Let's go home."

22

A Christmas Tale

The Thompson family made its annual trek over the farm yesterday in search of just the right Christmas tree.

Since we moved to the farm, we've made it a family outing. It's done on a Saturday morning and everyone participates.

The trips are always eventful. Not only does it help us all get into the Christmas spirit, it usually takes a couple of hours to find a tree we all can agree on.

It seems we always pick a tree that is too large for the house. Why is it that trees standing out in the middle of a cedar thicket always look a lot smaller than they actually are? It was no different yesterday in that respect, but some past tree-cutting trips have been more exciting.

As we discussed the annual outing a few days ago, the weather was unseasonably warm. Joe dryly commented, "I sure hope it's cold when we go get the tree."

"Why?" I wanted to know.

"It was warm last year and remember what happened?"

It was warm last year, and, yes, I do remember what happened. And, yes again, I am thankful it was cold this year.

Remembering the trip last year almost made me forego the trip this year.

It took me a good half hour to find a saw to cut the tree; it seems the boys are constantly reorganizing my tools.

The saw search somewhat soured my otherwise festive mood. And the one I finally found, a bow saw, had an annoying habit of spitting out the blade at the most inopportune moment— usually the moment I started to cut something with it.

Finally, we took to the woods. Matt wanted the first tree we came to. Of course, it was about thirty feet tall. By the time we explained to Matt his choice would be too big for the White House lawn, Joe had picked out three trees for us to choose from. They were only slightly smaller than Matt's choice.

Linda found a suitable one, until she noticed a bare space on one side. I convinced her that out of the several hundred trees we had to choose from there was surely a better specimen.

We decided to walk to another field where the trees are generally smaller and thicker.

We were surveying the trees and not really paying close attention to where we walked. As we wound our way down a narrow path, Joe shouted, "Look out, Dad! It's a snake!"

Every Tennessee country boy knows snakes aren't out in December. And I know most snakes won't hurt me, but a surprise encounter might make me hurt myself. I looked down. There, right in front of me, was a five-foot snake, lying lazily in the warm sun. I was surprised, to put it mildly.

I cleanly cleared two sizable cedars and a small dogwood and laid waste to a brier patch before banking high on the steep side of a gully. Then I accelerated to a blur on a flat stretch. Linda said that the second time I passed her, I actually looked rather sleek.

I finally stopped about a hundred yards away as my adrenaline supply ran out. I was streaming sweat, gasping for breath and spewing profanity. The bow saw was lodged in a treetop a good 50 yards away.

As my trembling subsided and the laughter died down, Joe spoke up again, "Boy, Daddy, I sure hope Santa Claus didn't hear what you said. If he did he'll stay at the North Pole."

Sure, Joe. There're no snakes at the North Pole.

23

Birthday's a Tough
Act for Swallow

Birthdays are special. They should be happy, fun and memorable occasions.

Sandy Morris, a family friend and neighbor, won't soon forget her nineteenth birthday. She'll still be talking about it years from now.

It was to be a special day. Sandy had a date. They planned a small private celebration. She specifically had instructed her family not to plan anything special. But when the big day came around everything else came apart.

First of all, the date never showed up. Being stood up is no way to celebrate number nineteen; Sandy called our daughter, Niki, and told her what happened. Niki immediately invited her to our house for a birthday celebration.

Upon Sandy's arrival, and after a vocal and animated discussion of the fellow who didn't show, Niki and Sandy went off to the kitchen to bake a birthday cake. They were determined to celebrate. Sandy seemed to be feeling better.

But it just wasn't meant to be.

From out of nowhere, a small bird appeared in the house. It flew from room to room with our sons Joe and Matt and the cat in hot pursuit. Every time Matt came close to the bird, it flew.

Every time he came close to the cat, it flew, too. The cat and Matt have a long-standing feud.

At first the chase was confined to the first-floor rooms. Linda was shouting for a cessation of the pursuit. Her pleas either went unheard, which is unlikely, or unheeded, which is probable. Meanwhile, the bird and the cat were going crazy.

After a brief chase through the upstairs rooms, the bird led the entourage back to the first floor. Sandy and Niki were busy mixing the cake and discussing, or cussin', old No Show.

The oven was preheated. Everything seemed to be going smoothly, but it just wasn't meant to be. Just as the cake was of the proper consistency to be poured into the pan, the chase came through the kitchen again. With the boys and the cat gaining on it, the bird desperately sought refuge.

None of us will ever know what the bird thought it was, but for some unexplained reason it took a dive—right into the cake batter. It came out full bore, wings flapping and struggling, flinging cake batter about the room like dry leaves in a whirlwind.

Joe and Matt were giggling. Linda was still shouting. Niki and Sandy were screaming. The dripping bird was flying in circles. And the cat looked very confused.

We may be forced to put the cat into therapy.

Finally, the bird once again sought refuge near the girls. It flew onto Niki's sweater and immediately entangled its claws in the loose weave of the fabric. Then the bird started screaming, or screeching, or whatever birds do when they're struggling for survival in a hostile atmosphere. Niki is believed to have had a religious experience. At least those near her swear she spoke in tongues.

Once untangled, the bird cautiously perched on Niki's shoulder. She also managed to calm the boys and run them out of the kitchen while she mopped up the cake batter. Seeing a bird perched on Niki's shoulder only served to further confuse the cat.

The bird roosted on the headboard of Niki's bed all night long. Early the next morning, before Matt or the cat woke up,

Joe managed to coax the bird to fly to freedom out an upstairs window. I'll bet it hasn't stopped since.

I asked Sandy if I could use her name when I wrote about her birthday *celebration*.

"Sure," she said, "and you can use the guy's name too. It's spelled J-e-r-k."

Although Sandy didn't have her date with J-e-r-k, or a birthday cake, she certainly had a memorable birthday. And somewhere in the vast outdoors—probably many, many, miles away—there's a bird that'll remember it too.

And the cat? Well, when she sees a bird on television now, she goes into a convulsive spasm.

24

Saying "I Love You!"

Many people are still searching for a perfect mate.

Check the classified ads in the newspapers, magazines or the grocery store tabloids, and you'll agree with me that a phenomenal number of people are looking for other people.

What worries me is that the people who place the ads avoid the word *love* like the plague. Instead they talk about seeking "companionship," a "meaningful relationship," a "swinging time," and sometimes "possibly marriage."

But never love.

What is it about love that makes people afraid to call it love? I love a lot of people and a lot of things. I'm not bashful. I tell Linda I love her. I tell the kids. I tell even the Budweiser man.

Some people may feel it's too much of a commitment to say it. Maybe they worry that they will get hurt.

When I first started dating, my dad warned me not to tell a girl I loved her. "You'll have played your hole card," he said. "She'll control you from then on."

Fortunately, Mother's advice was the opposite. She knew, of course, that when it came to poker—or loving her—Dad never was much on hiding his hole card.

Noah Webster defines *love* as "a deep affection or liking for someone or something." I understand that. What I can't understand, is people who feel it but won't say it. Life isn't tennis. In tennis, *love* means nothing. Zero. In life it means everything.

I'm fortunate to have found someone who is about as near perfect as is humanly possible. She tells me frequently she loves me. So I'm lucky in love.

Still, I keep looking for ways to test Linda's love. Of course, she says being married to me, in itself, has been a ten-year test. Great sense of humor, that Linda.

If you are looking for ways to test love, get yourself a copy of *The Old Farmer's Almanac.* In it you'll find "56 surefire techniques for finding, attracting, and wedding the person you will love forever."

There was this test: "Cut a lemon in half, rub both pieces on the four corners of your bed, then sleep with the lemon halves under your pillow. If you see the one you love in a dream, he or she will be faithful to you. If you don't dream of the one you love, he or she will be unfaithful."

I followed the instructions meticulously. I even squeezed the lemons flat so they wouldn't make a hump under Linda's pillow. I waited anxiously the next morning for just the right minute to ask about her dream.

She did have a delightful dream, she said. It was about broiled flounder. She won't have to worry about the fidelity of a broiled flounder.

This was another of the "56 ways": "Eat a thimbleful of salt before going to bed. Whoever brings you water in your dreams will be your lover."

Tough luck, Linda. I hope it doesn't hurt too much when I run off with three waterpersons for the Vanderbilt football team.

Well, the third time is supposed to be a charm. This is what the *Almanac* recommended: "Pick an apple, prick it full of holes. Carry it for a while under your left arm, then give it to your lover."

It's supposed to attract her to you forever.

I tried it Sunday. I stashed it under my arm while Ernest

Angley was doing his TV healing. I kept it there through two NFL football games and the Sunday night television movie, *I Dream of Jeannie, 15 Years Later.*

Then I gave it to Linda just before the ten o'clock news.

You know I think it worked. She swooned. She grew faint. Her voice trembled. She was short of breath. She was so overcome with emotion she could hardly talk.

Ain't love grand?

PART FOUR
Philosophies and Observations

25

On Mice and Women

I was still in bed yesterday morning when Linda started down the stairs. I heard her scream. A few minutes later, Tanya went down the steps. She screamed, too.

Normally, such screams would jar me from the bed rushing to check the extent of injuries. Not this time. I knew immediately what the problem was. I heard the words *damn cat* interjected in both screams. I just pulled up the covers and cussed the cat, too.

Sapphire, out trusty and faithful cat, had struck again. She had murdered a little mouse. When she murders mice, she always brings the lifeless bodies to the bottom of the steps. She wants to make sure the first thing we see in the morning is her fresh kill of the night before. Or maybe she just wants to hear Linda and Tanya scream.

Not many things frighten Linda. She's not even afraid of snakes. Or dogs. Or me. She's actually fond of dogs and snakes. And, since she has on occasion equated me with both, I accuse her of being a little fond of me, too.

Several years ago, she brought two pet rat snakes from a co-worker's home and set them free in our barn. They may still be there. I don't know because I haven't been in the barn in several years.

When Linda saw the huge snapping turtle Joe and Matt brought in the house on New Year's Eve, she calmly said, "My goodness boys, that may be the biggest, meanest snapping turtle I've ever seen. Please take it back outside."

So why then, does she scream and cuss the cat when she finds a puny little dead mouse at the foot of the stairs?

But it's not just Linda. Beverly Burnett, a secretary here at *The Tennessean*, jumped flat-footed from the floor to her chair recently as a small mouse scampered across the floor. She immediately ordered several traps.

And, Rose Palermo, a local attorney, is outspoken when she discusses mice, "I hate the little bastards. They are vicious."

More than once, Rose, who is fearless in court, has been known to take to her desk top at the sight of a mouse.

"The first time it happened," she says, "I was with a client. This woman was in my office pouring out her heart. She was getting a divorce. She was looking to me as her tower of strength—the means through which she could rescue her life. She just casually mentioned: 'Look, a mouse.' Immediately, I was on top of my desk screaming. I don't know what the woman thought.

"The next time, I was again talking with a woman about a divorce. She had another woman with her. They had their backs to the mouse, but I saw it run across the floor between me and my secretary. In a split second. I was on the desk top again screaming. I'll never forget the look on their faces."

I think mice are unnecessarily maligned. I can't understand why a person weighing more than a hundred pounds can be afraid of a cute, fuzzy little animal that weighs probably no more than an ounce or two.

First of all, mice do not attack. Given the chance they will run from a person. They don't bark, or snarl or growl. Even if they did bite, how much could it hurt? Surely such a tiny animal could do no more than pinch.

I'm sure some people who scream and take evasive action at the sight of a mouse wouldn't hesitate to reach out and pet a pit bulldog or a Doberman, two hombres that can put a real bite on you.

The only time Linda screams is when she finds dead mice, or live mice. But it's kinda like the story of the little boy who cried wolf too often. Someday she might trot down the stairs and find something really worth screaming about. Like an escapee from the mental hospital, standing nude in the living room with a bloody ax.

She'd probably really scream then.

And I'd probably just pull up the covers and cuss the cat.

26

Horoscopes

I am amazed at the number of people who read their daily horoscope in the morning paper and take it seriously.

They won't wear red, will cancel a business appointment, won't eat vegetables, and might even go back to bed if the "stars" tell them to beware on a given day.

That's silly business.

Superstition should be made of smarter stuff. I'd sooner run from a black cat than take a horoscope seriously.

But the horoscope is a great hustle.

Last week I was in Atlanta and tuned in the motel's television set to a cable channel. All you had to do was dial a 900 number, pay a 50-cent toll charge and give your birthdate to find out what an astrologer said were your chances of living, dying, falling in love, having sex, having your children kidnapped, making a fortune, or losing your job.

That can cost a real believer in star gazing $15 a month.

Not me.

But I have noticed that the signs of the Zodiac can be powerful conversation-starters.

I first noticed this back in my single days during a visit to a bar in New York City.

This fellow sitting near me turned to a beautiful young woman next to him and said, "I'll bet you are a Leo. I can tell by the pensive look in those big, brown eyes that you are a deep thinker."

He was so obvious that I snickered and waited for the echo when she slapped his face. It never came. She told him how perceptive he was, and within a few minutes they were laughing and talking like the dearest of friends.

Another fellow had a slightly different approach.

He just asked outright, "What's your sign?"

The woman he had never seen before smiled and told him she was a Pisces. I watched with envy as he moved in and they were lost in happy chatter.

So a few more drinks and I'm thinking, "What the hell, Thompson, you at least know your own sign. Use it." So I turn to the lovely lady on my right and I say. "My dear, I'll bet you are a Cancer."

"And I'll bet you've got it," she cracked and left.

Discouraged, but undaunted, I glanced to my left to another lovely lady several seats away. I smiled at her. She smiled back.

Reeking with nonchalance, I moved casually down and took the seat next to her.

I smiled again. So did she, I knew exactly what to say:

"What's your sign?"

"It's $150, and I can take American Express."

"What's your sign?" she asked.

"Broke," I said—and left.

When I got to my room I checked the newspaper.

My horoscope said, "Don't talk to strangers today and you won't be disappointed."

Coincidence. Sheer coincidence.

To prove it. I've been looking at the horoscopes of the last few days and the advice they offer is ridiculous.

Last Saturday, for instance, if you are a Taurus: "Avoid a new contact in the evening." Taurus types are known for dull evenings.

Leos were told: "Tonight, avoid work of all kind."

That's impossible, Leos are workaholics. And I sure hope we didn't have any policemen, firemen, cab drivers, pilots, doctors or nurses who were Leos.

Pisces were told: "Enjoy solitude this evening." That's fine, but some Pisces, like some of the rest of us, don't enjoy solitude at bedtime.

Today my horoscope tells me to "Be with persons who are practical . . . and forget the emotional ones who can be upsetting."

Nothing I can do about it. I'm meeting this morning with the newspaper's publisher, who wants me to do more columns every week.

He's not very practical and is bound to get emotional about it. But, again, what the hell. I think the whole thing is ridiculous. I personally don't believe in horoscopes.

That's a trait of us Cancers you know.

27

Spring Fever

Someone once said that in the spring a young man's fancy turns to love.

I don't know who said it, but they knew what they were talking about. They could've even taken it a step further and said spring affects older men the same way. I speak from experience.

Linda knows she's my first love. Secure in this knowledge, she tolerates my infatuations from time to time. I'm glad I'm not too old for my fancy to turn to love, because for the past few days I've felt it happening. I've had that certain gleam in my eye. I've been a little restless. A little jittery. And a lot romantic.

I'm fully aware of what's happening. I'm infatuated again. I get this way every year about this time. And, I'm not blind to the fact that the object of my infatuation is flirtatious and fickle.

I don't mind the flirtatious part. In fact, I kinda like it. It's the fickle part I could forego. You see, I'm infatuated with spring.

At 4:03 p.m. today, spring officially arrives in Middle Tennessee. Ray Burgess, a forecaster for the U.S. Weather Service, said it's expected to be cloudy and cold with the temperature rising to only about 40 degrees.

So, the first day of spring doesn't necessarily coincide with the first spring day.

Still I think spring is wonderful. And spring has mastered the art of flirting. Just when spring lulls you into a sense of comfort, bathed in warm sunshine, caressed by the aroma of fresh blossoms and soothed by the lilting melodies of songbirds, watch out. Spring can be very fickle. Harsh sometimes.

My plum tree is in full bloom. What a beautiful sight. Clouds of white blossoms set against a dull background of winter's brown. But I know from past experience not to trust spring to protect the tender blossoms, and later, the young plums.

For the past three years, the tree has been laden with blooms. And for the past three years, spring has sneaked in a late freeze or heavy frost to prevent any plum picking at my house. Since the temperature is expected to dip into the upper teens tonight, spring won't keep me in suspense this year.

However, a romantic refuses to be dissuaded by reality. Oh my, how quickly we forget. We never remember the harshness or fickleness. Just as we never forget the gentle caress of a warm, morning breeze. Or the smell of fresh-turned earth. The first crocus. The first buttercup. The birds singing as if to welcome the new season with a symphony.

I feel a rush of enthusiasm each day as I watch the subtle changes taking place in the hills and valleys between home and work. The brown hills of winter gradually melting into the beautiful green of spring.

Spring also brings grass to cut, weeds to pull from the roses. And always accompanying my dear, sweet spring are insects and ticks. I found my first tick last weekend.

Spring has a certain mystique. It can cause people to be enthusiastic and full of energy one minute. And the next minute they'll be staring off into space with a blank look on their face. Oh, it's an illness all right. It's Spring Fever. And, like many illnesses, it just has to run its course. It doesn't pick its victims. It's a peril to old and young, male and female. Little boys get it. Joe and Matt have already caught it. They've displayed all the symptoms. They probably caught it from their dad.

There will always be a warm spot in my heart to greet the arrival of spring. Because spring brings something no other season can match. Something every country boy looks forward to, yearns for. Something that makes my heart flutter when I find it.

Spring brings poke sallet. Pure nectar. Finding a new patch of poke sallet is like finding a box of chocolates at a Weight Watchers meeting.

Poke sallet is the most compelling reason I love spring.

Linda may be a little jealous of poke sallet.

28

When Words Hide the Truth

T_he Tennessean_ has a policy that prohibits the use of most four-letter words.

It's not a policy we all agree with all the time, but it is one we live with all the time.

Some words, although not acceptable for newspaper usage, are universally descriptive. And journalists often need a word to describe the misleading verbiage often put out by politicians, bureaucrats and professionals.

A single descriptive word that immediately comes to mind is b—s—t, more commonly referred to as b.s. Country boy and city boy alike know what it smells like, and both readily recognize it.

For example, politicians don't like to talk about raising taxes. They will vote, however, for "revenue enhancement." Now, that's b.s. Revenue enhancement does the same thing that raising taxes does—it takes money from my paycheck.

Many car lots have abandoned the label "used" as it refers to its cars. Now their cars are "pre-owned." It makes no difference whether they have been "pre-owned" by one person or a dozen, it's still a used car. To call it anything else is b.s.

I've known some pretty interesting used car salesmen, but I

can't think of a single pre-owned car salesman that wasn't boring as all get out.

Some supermarkets have sections of their produce departments set aside for "distressed produce." I remember when distressed meant pain or suffering and bruised or rotten described the condition of fruits and vegetables. Or someone else's kids.

Then there are some subjects people almost refuse to talk about. And when they are forced to, they deliberately try to confuse the issue.

Death is such a subject.

When I was a child, grown-ups would talk about someone "passing" or "passing away." Apparently those terms were easier to deal with than a person dying. When I was the police beat reporter for *The Tennessean*, I covered wrecks, shootings, disasters and all sorts of other things that resulted in death.

Yet when I called the local hospitals to check on the conditions of people involved in these things, I can't remember once being told they had died. They had expired.

Hospitals still shun death and dying, yet many have stopped using the term *expired*. Now, they describe death as "negative patient outcome." But when Dr. Charles Harlan, Metro's medical examiner, fills out his report, it's strictly nuts and bolts. He doesn't note the time of negative patient outcome, he jots down the time of death.

Gretel Harlan, the medical examiner's wife, is also a doctor. She is confronted regularly with the various ways hospitals still refuse to acknowledge death for what it really is.

"They rarely say 'die,'" she said, "but there's little doubt about it when the chart reads 'discharged to morgue.' Other charts may say that 'CPR [cardio-pulmonary resuscitation] failed,' or that the patient was 'found with no vital signs.' They mean the same thing, of course. The patient has died."

Good for you, doctors Harlan.

My fishing license expires this year, but for $10.50 I can give it new life. Death is final. It sounds final.

I've always had a fondness for Benjamin Franklin. He was a

newspaperman, too. He sometimes ran risque stories on his front page. While he would never explicitly use the word b— s—t, you can take bets that he, too, knew what it smelled like.

I kinda wish he were alive today. He would have a ball with some of the new words and terminology.

I can almost see the twinkle in his eyes as he looks over his little wire-rimmed glasses and spouts something profound, something like, "Nothing in life is certain except negative patient outcome and revenue enhancement."

Electrifying, Ben. Electrifying.

29

On Being Lost

If you've ever been lost, I'm sure you remember it.

I was about five years old when I first got lost. It was at the old Tennessee Central Railway Station at the foot of Nashville's Broadway.

My mother had taken my little brother Ronnie, who was two, and me there to catch a train to Oak Ridge where Dad was working.

Suddenly I found myself separated from mother and Ronnie.

I was terrified. I was alone for the first time in a strange place. I broke into tears.

Several people came to my rescue.

Then I heard my name on the loudspeaker. I remember the frantic look on Mother's face as she made her way through the crowd.

Things have changed a lot in four decades. No longer are there crowds at railroad stations in Nashville. Union Station is a hotel, the Tennessee Central Terminal was razed. The Thermal Transfer Plan now occupies the site.

People have changed, too.

Many of us are now afraid to help anybody, even a crying child. A fellow told me the other day that there have been so many child abuse stories in the media that he felt it safer to keep away from kids who are lost. What are we coming to?

Just recently, at the Longhorn Championship Rodeo, Matt, who is four, got separated from the rest of us. Our daughters, Niki and Tanya, went in opposite directions in Municipal Auditorium looking for him.

When they found him, he was just like I had been so long ago. Terrified, he was sitting in the middle of the walkway crying. The crowd walked around him, ignoring him. Not one offered to help.

Just like me, he will remember for the rest of his life getting lost.

But getting lost is not just for little kids.

I've been lost since. Once as a teen-ager, 'possum hunting at night, I wandered lost for three hours before I saw a house light and followed it to safety. I was older, stronger, more secure. But I can remember those last 30 minutes as being filled with fears that I would not be able to find my way. I might starve. Or die of thirst.

Recently, while Joe, Matt and I were driving down a lonely stretch of road in Humphreys County, we came upon a man with a cloth bag in his hand. He was an adult who knew the area. But he was totally lost. And scared.

He had lived around there for all his years. When we stopped to ask if we could help him he said, "Mister, I'm lost, can you tell me where I am?" I wanted to tell him that you are never lost when you don't know where you are. You are only lost when you don't know where you are going. But his fright made me refrain from what Linda calls my half-witted humor.

We gave him a lift to where he had left his car. He had walked for 25 miles. No wonder that look in his eyes reminded me of times I have been lost.

He told us, "Every time I would think I was going the right way back in those woods, I would talk myself out of it. When a feller is lost, his mind just don't work right, you know it?" How well I know.

The last time I was lost I was piloting my plane on a trip to

Iowa. Now that is a lonely feeling. I knew I was south of my true course. I remembered some advice I had been given by an old airport bum who said, "Never rely on your instincts when you think you are lost. Always rely on your instruments."

When you are flying alone, your only friends are instruments.

This time my friends didn't let me down.

But I worry about a world where instruments reach out a helping hand, but human beings won't.

30

On Grandparents and Grandchildren

Some preachers can talk for hours without really saying anything a person will remember, and some can preach a sermon that has a lasting impact.

Not long ago, Nashville businessman Jim Blevins was touched by a sermon he heard in Florida.

In fact, he's given it a lot of thought and energy. He wasn't spiritually reawakened, nor did he rededicate his life or speak in tongues or anything like that. It wasn't that kind of sermon. It was a sermon on grandparents.

"That sermon really hit home," Blevins said. "It was especially meaningful for me because I've never known a grandfather. I don't even know what they looked like. I barely remember my father. He died when I was ten."

Some of the things the preacher, Dr. Richard M. Cromie, minister of the First Presbyterian Church in Fort Lauderdale, Florida, talked about were things grandparents should do.

Right off the bat, Cromie was confronted by a member of his church who wanted to know what gave him the authority to tell grandparents what they should do when he was not yet a grandparent. He said this confrontation brought back immediate memories of his preaching professors who admonished,

"Never try to handle topics you do not know about first hand. Tell them what you know."

So, relying on his experience as a grandchild, Brother Cromie went on with his sermon.

The preacher related the story of Jacob calling his son, Joseph, to his death bed to discuss important things and to talk about funeral arrangements. Then, he had some advice for grandparents.

He said they must make themselves available to their grandchildren. The new style of aging, he said, sometimes makes this difficult by placing tremendous emphasis on the independence of the older generation.

Grandparents today, he told his congregation, sometime fail to accept the hard work, or take the time and effort, to overcome the distance of the generations and the miles which could separate them. He urged them to make their granchildren feel special, noting that hardly anyone writes to children anymore, and grandfathers almost never do.

The preacher got Jim Blevins thinking. Since then, he has taken it a few steps further and has made a list of things he plans to do for his grandchildren. He urges other grandparents to do likewise.

"Grandparents lucky enough to know their grandchildren should keep things," Blevins said. "They may seem insignificant at the time, and they may be meaningless to the grandchild when they're young, but as they grow older, just regular things take on a special meaning.

"I'm speaking of anything from their parents, their family tree, photo albums, a family history. Anything they've made with their hands. Any newspaper clippings in which they're mentioned, trophies they may have won, awards they received. All these things will be tremendously important to grandchildren when they're old enough to wonder about, and appreciate, their heritage.

"And they should write a narrative of their life story. There's no one better suited, or more knowledgeable. It doesn't have to be a literary masterpiece, just their life story in their own words. I'd give anything if I had some of these things from my grandparents. People should feel they're establishing their own individual time capsule."

Blevins is doing these things for his grandchildren. He's placed several articles in a steel storage safe at his business and plans to make several more such safes available for others wishing to do the same thing.

It gives me a certain satisfaction, too, knowing he's saving all these things. Long after we're both gone, I can just hear someone saying, "Wonder who this Thompson fellow was? Sounds like he knew our grandpa."

PART FIVE
On Food

31

Scat, Temptation!

A lot of people would agree that the world has more than an ample supply of temptation. It's just that some people handle it better than others.

I handle temptation very poorly.

To a person stranded in the middle of the desert, a large glass of cool water would be tempting.

Try to imagine the temptation presented by a boatload of women paddling toward a sailor in the middle of a desert island.

As I said, I handle temptation very poorly. I did start off with great enthusiasm and a strong intent. I started walking daily, watching what I ate and especially what I drank. The pounds started coming off. I was so proud of myself.

Then temptation overtook my progress and I did what preachers are always chastising us for and warning us against— I backslid.

One of the most vivid examples I can recall is Cousin Elmore. Of course he had fewer temptations in his day than I have to deal with today. His major temptation was the demon rum.

He decided to do something about it. He went to a religious service at which the preacher healed people. Cousin Elmore accepted the invitation and bared his life, and his weakness for the bottle, to the entire crowd.

The next day he was a changed man. We all agreed he even looked better—that he looked as if a giant burden had been lifted from his shoulders. Cousin Elmore said he could feel the warm spirit of resistance coursing through his body. He said he felt much better since he quit drinking.

So, based on the experience of Cousin Elmore, I know there's hope for me. It may take a spiritual awakening to make me decline homemade ice cream in the future. Or it may just take a new resolve to refuse to give in to temptation in any form. But I'll do it.

Cousin Elmore's new-found conversion to the good life of living without strong drink lasted only about three weeks. Yes, he, too, backslid. He must have tired of feeling and looking so good because he returned to the bottle and didn't return to any more tent meetings.

However, Cousin Elmore did finally quit the bottle for good—proof that no situation is hopeless.

And when he quit we all agreed that he sure looked natural.

32

Don't Measure Me at the Waist!

When I started flying airplanes, I got some sage advice on a navigation problem from an old pilot buddy.

"Well, lad," he began, "there's one thing to keep in mind. You can never figure out where you're going until you first determine where you are."

That tidbit of wisdom has served me well in the cockpit. It's also appropriate in other areas.

I have no idea, for instance, where I'm going with my fledgling fitness regimen until I first determine where I am. Enter the *Reader's Digest* Guide to Family Fitness.

The first phase of the fitness guide seeks to determine, "How fit are you?"

"By taking the *Reader's Digest* Fitness Test you can find out in 15 minutes how fit you are compared with other Americans," it begins.

The first measurement is to determine how much fat is on the body. It gives instructions for women, men, and children.

A woman is instructed to measure around her hips at the widest part. Then she is to locate her "hip girth" and her height in inches on the chart. The connecting line between the two will determine the percentage of her body fat. Less than 18 percent is excellent and scores five points.

The minute I saw the instructions for the man, I knew the test was rigged. It wouldn't allow me to measure my hip girth at the widest part. No siree. I had to really be tested.

"Measure the circumference of your waist at the navel. Then use the chart as above to determine body fat."

I made the required measurements. When I attempted to connect the line between my height and my body weight, it went off the scale.

So much for the first phase. I didn't score. On to the next one, curl-ups.

"The number of curl-ups you can do in one minute is an effective measure of the muscular strength and endurance of your abdominal muscles. A strong abdomen will help you avoid low-back pain and maintain good posture."

Again, I suspected the test was fixed. It favors robust, young, slender jet setters. You know the kind. You've seen 'em on television. They smile a lot, stand by the fireplace in deep conversation, and sip white wine.

"Lie flat on your back with knees bent, and heels twelve to eighteen inches from the buttocks," the instructions begin.

First of all, anyone who can lie down with their heels twelve inches from their buttocks already has a strong abdomen. And skinny legs. They probably also have excruciating low-back pain. I probably couldn't lie flat on my back and get my heels within twelve inches of someone else's buttocks.

I took another no-score and moved to the next test—push-ups.

It was during the push-ups test that I copped my first score. I got a one. Anyone in my age bracket, 40–49, who manages to perform between 0 to 11 push-ups in one minute scores one point. I perfomed in that range.

I scored again on the next one—the sit and reach test. This one starts by sitting on the floor with your legs extended in front of you and your feet touching a wall. If you can reach the wall and slap your palms flat against it, you get an excellent rating and five points. If, however, your fingertips are four or more inches from your toes, you get a lousy score, but you still score a point. Mine were. But I scored. I have extremely short fingers.

Since I almost collapsed after one minute of the three-minute step-test, I took a no-score there, too.

But I did score two points. Now I know where I'm going because I know where I am.

I am going to begin stretching exercises. I'll work toward being taller.

According to the *Reader's Digest* charts, it's not that I'm so much overweight. I'm just not tall enough.

33

The Fiber-Filled Diet

For some time I've been planning to start a diet. Not that I'm actually starting it, I'm still investigating the right diet for me.

My wife Linda, a follower of the late J. I. Rodale, health food guru, has been trying to push the investigation along.

She keeps quoting *Prevention* and *Organic Gardening*, both of which are magazines created by the late J. I. Rodale.

Until she told me, I thought *Prevention* was a birth control publication and that *Organic Gardening* had to do with sex in the tall corn.

But Linda swears by the late J. I.

The late J. I. was strong on fiber. So is Linda. She makes her own granola and will eat it as cereal with doses of raw honey. She has a passion for miller's bran. She is big on fresh fruit and vegetables. If you like broccoli, asparagus, apricots, and prunes you can be a hero at my house. And yogurt. Yuk!

I believe in household harmony, so I listen to Linda's sermons and her quotations from the late J. I.

I refrain, most often, from reminding her that the late J. I. dropped dead in 1971 immediately after an appearance on the Dick Cavett show during which he said, "I'm so healthy I expect to live on and on."

It is not unusual at my house for Linda to tell me that Orientals live longer because they eat a lot of rice.

She will read me a quotation like this one, "Cultures whose diets are unprocessed and natural have little incidence of heart disease."

I refrain, most often, from telling her that cave men ate exactly the sort of diet the late J. I. recommends: raw fruits, high fiber, and bulk—all unprocessed, natural, no additives or preservatives. And the average life span of a cave man was 31 years.

When Linda starts feeding me those foods recommended by the late J. I., I get to feeling like she is getting our car ready for a MARTA emissions inspections.

I know I have a taste for foods I was raised on.

Bacon and eggs, hot biscuits and jam, sometimes with hash browns and grits for breakfast. A hot dog or cheeseburger for lunch, with fries or chili, washed down by a long-neck Pepsi. And at supper, something more substantial like steak or roast beef and potatoes with homemade pie for dessert. And all of it with scalding black coffee.

I admit there are quirks in my diet. For example, I'm a liver lover. People think that's weird. Even my mother thought she had raised a strange child when she discovered I liked liver.

She didn't like liver, but nutrition experts who preceded the late J. I. said it would put iron in your blood and make you live longer.

Now nutrition experts say that liver is high in harmful cholesterol and is a storehouse for all the awful things the animal ate before it made the supreme sacrifice. But I like to eat what I like, not what the late J. I. says I should like. The late J. I. never knew the fabulous taste of turnip greens or the tasty tang of pork barbecue, and he would have hated souse.

J. I. helped turn staples like milk and eggs into no-no's. Cholesterol. As J. I. would say—had he survived his own heart failure—cholesterol will clog up your blood vessels, cause heart problems and pay for condos in the Caribbean for heart surgeons.

So I sat down to table recently and expressed surprise when my beloved Linda, the devoted disciple of the late J. I., put ham salad sandwiches in front of me.

I was elated. I had expected alfalfa sprouts and carrot juice.

"Why do I rate ham salad?" I asked tentatively.

"It's high in fiber."

"Come on, there's no fiber in ham."

"There is in yours. I dropped a wooden spoon in the blender."

Eat your heart out, J. I.

34

The Joy of Poke Sallet

May is one of my more favorite times of the year—poke sallet time.

For years many people have looked forward to the emergence of the poke plant. They drool over its delicious flavor and anticipate that first big mess of sallet.

I've always been fascinated with poke sallet. And that's what it is around here, but in some areas of the world it's known officially as poke weed. It's long been a mysterious plant.

Early settlers used the root of the plant for medicinal purposes. They learned, probably from the native Indians, that poke root eased the pain of arthritis. The poke stalk split and rubbed on poison ivy rash dries it right up. They also used the dark-colored berries in homemade dyes.

But they also learned poke sallet is delicious, and as a result it occupied a prominent place on springtime tables. And for many of us, it still does.

I think when the early settlers first found out all the good things associated with poke sallet, they deliberately started the nasty rumor that the plant is poisonous. I don't know why it was started, but whatever the reason, I've never heard of anyone being poisoned by poke sallet.

Just as the plant has always fascinated me, Dr. Maurice Edwards, professor of biology at the University of Tennessee-Chattanooga, shares my fascination. He has applied for a federal grant to conduct research into the medicinal qualities of poke sallet.

"There are many references in medical literature that poke sallet is beneficial for arthritis treatment," Edwards said. "We've learned enough already that a scientific journal has accepted an article for publication. This department and some undergraduate students have been doing research on poke sallet since 1982. We also know that in South America some tribal witchdoctors use poke as a healing potion.

"Our research has disclosed that poke berry juice can inhibit the germination and sprouting of its own seed in addition to the seeds of other plants. This is known as auto-toxicity. This allows the plant to do away with its competition through herbal warfare.

"As early as 1974, medical research found some extract from the root of poke that was used in leukemia research. A compound from poke was discovered that causes white blood cells to divide.

"Another poke compound has demonstrated an ability to inhibit the polio virus from growing in tissue cells in the laboratory. In the last five and a half years, over 2,000 articles have mentioned poke, according to a computer search. So, the research is continuing. We know AIDS is caused by a virus and who knows, maybe there's something in poke sallet that will inhibit this one too? It definitely deserves further exploration.

"But whatever is found in the future, I already know it's delicious. I had my first mess last week."

Discussing the medical aspects of poke sallet reminded me of a day years ago in the waiting room at St. Thomas Hospital where my grandmother was hospitalized. It was in the spring and we overheard a woman talking to a friend about poke sallet. I'll never forget how tickled my mother got.

"I'll tell you, about the worst I ever hurt was years ago after I eat a big bait of poke sallet," the woman told her friend. "The pain in my stomach was so bad I just doubled over.

"I thought I was going to die before the doctor got there. He didn't do a thing but ask me what I'd had for dinner, and I told him about the big bait of poke sallet. He said I was eating too much grease.

"I told him it couldn't 'a been that 'cause I just put one rabbit in it."

PART SIX
Modern Irritations

35

Needed: More, Better "Johns"

There are some things people don't like to talk about. Going to the bathroom is one of them.

I have small children, and it seems they always have to go. When we're together, I spend a lot of time looking for bathrooms. I suspect all parents have gone through the same thing.

Sheri Reynolds of Kingston Springs has. She even wrote a column about some of her problems. Better yet, she sent it to me. I'll share some of her frustrations.

"Talking about going to the bathroom is a taboo subject," Sheri wrote. "Admit it, it's embarrassing. You're visiting someone or at a party, and you gotta go. There's always a note of apology in your voice when you ask directions.

"How many times have you sat in the plane and waited? Everyone knows what you're going to do if you get up and walk down the aisle.

"Do you ever go to the movies, drink a jumbo coke, can't stand to miss any of the show, and try to go before you leave for home? Might as well go home. There's always a line a mile long. And what do you do while you wait in line? Look at the floor, talk about the movie, stare at the ceiling or check to see if there really are feet in that last stall?

"How about those new Kroger super stores? You can buy a radio, rent a movie, check out the best sellers, eat supper and pick up a dozen red roses for the wife. But you can't go to the bathroom. The double doors to the 'john' say 'Employees Only.' Unless you're holding the hand of a small child, you're not likely to enter.

"You haven't lived until you go to the bathroom at the Atlanta airport with two kids. Try sitting down with a baby in a snugli, two carry-ons, a diaper bag, purse, wet floor and a four-year-old that crawls under and locks the next door from inside.

"Although this seems to be written from a woman's perspective, I know some guys who would give their three-star bad rating to the men's room at the old Vandy stadium. Something about spraying a concrete wall."

Say no more, Sheri. I'm a believer. I've been there. It seems stores and shopping malls deliberately try to conceal their "public" restrooms from the public.

Drive-in markets do, too. I'd call them convenience stores, but I can't in good conscience. A store that hides its bathroom is an inconvenience store. On several occasions, I've asked to use the bathroom in a drive-in market only to be told "we don't have one." I always ask where they go. Then I watch them squirm, too.

More than once, I've been told by liquor store clerks I couldn't use their bathroom because "it's against the law." I know there are some funny laws on the books, but there's nothing funny about making it illegal to use the bathroom.

What if a person couldn't wait? What if they just barged on in? Would they be arrested? Would they go to jail? I'd sure hate to have something like that on my record. How could I ever tell my grandchildren I'd been thrown in the slammer on an illegal bathroom use charge?

Sheri said she'd like to see a movement started to get more and better restrooms built and opened to the public. She'd also like a directory or guide to "Public Restrooms in the Nashville Area."

I'd like to see similar information on road maps. There's nothing more frustrating than zipping along the interstate with a car full of squirming kids all needing to go. You spot a sign in the distance telling you how far it is to the rest area. It also says in big letters, "No Restroom." It makes me so mad, I usually let them void where prohibited.

Sheri says she'd welcome a campaign toward "More and Better Johns."

I seriously thought about approaching my publisher, John Seigenthaler, with this suggestion, but I had second thoughts. He'd surely say something smart alecky like, "I don't have time to discuss it right now. I've got to go to the Jerry."

36

Whatever Happened to Toys?

In the middle of the toy department of a Nashville department store yesterday, I had the feeling I was in another world.

I love toy departments. I'm thankful I have young children so I don't look out of place when I wander through one. When my kids get too old for toy departments, then I'll just look out of place.

In this toy department there were prehistoric-looking animals that change to modernistic space vehicles with laser cannons protruding from the wings.

I saw a large Castle Grayskull and Masters of the Universe action figures and a giant prehistoric animal skeleton called Battle Bones that holds up to a dozen of the action figures.

I once spent a lot of time in toy departments. Then the main toys were cowboy guns and stick horses and Slinkys and hula hoops. The cowboys always had white hats and the bad guys all wore black hats. The world was simple then.

The cowboys fought the bad guys over water for the widow's ranch and they always won. Not only did they get the water to the widow's thirsty cattle, they usually got the widow, too.

That's not the case now. I don't know who's good or who's

bad. I don't know what they're fighting about or who is supposed to win. Or, if they win, what they win.

I didn't see a single cowboy gun. Instead, I saw oversized houseflies. Big ugly ones. The Sectaur Flyers—Heroic Sectaur, Evil Sectaur, Pinsor, or Battle Beetle.

Nothing is what it seems anymore. Everything changes to something else. There's a Transformer electric train and battle set. The electric trains I knew and loved hauled wooden logs around a track and through a tunnel. I never got tired of hauling logs.

The electric trains today allow kids to "Command the power of the Transformers by changing each car of the Heroic Autobot Train to defeat evil." So much for hauling logs when there's evil to be defeated.

Then there's the Voltron Battling Black Lion. Kids are urged to "Watch as your Voltron Black Lion walks into battle. Flap its wings, wag its tail and raise his gun and your Voltron Lion is ready to defend the universe. Requires 2 AA batteries."

Somehow I figured a lion that has wings, raises a gun when it wags its tail, and defends the universe, would require more than just a cage and an occasional hunk of meat.

Here I was among the Decepticon planes, the Autobot cars, the Gobots, the Spydor and the Land Shark Vehicle that is half shark and half army tank.

Where was I when they created the Real Baby for less than $30? The one with the baby bottles and disposable diaper and five birth announcements and the one that comes with your choice of "Wide Eyed" or "Sleepy Baby." The one that doesn't keep you up nights and doesn't have to be fed.

The very thought of anyone paying thirty bucks for a baby when for a few bucks more they could have done the decent thing and adopted a Cabbage Patch Kid in the "16-inch regular, or 14-inch newborn" size—"adoption papers included."

After a rather exhaustive search, I left the world of universe defenders, evil fighters, and surrogate babies, and found myself back in the real world.

I found a See 'N Say—a real honest to goodness "The Farmer

Says See 'N Say"; My Little Pony; a Frisbee; Clippety-Clop the Wonder Horse; and even a Slinky.

"Excuse me," I said to a red-smocked clerk, "could you direct me to the hula hoops?"

"Gee, guy, I've never heard of 'em. You might check in automotive."

That clerk would never make it in the record department.

Probably thinks Guy Lombardo is a back ailment.

37

How About Tying on This One

I know men who for years have struggled to tie a necktie.

If they ever get one tied right, they never untie it. They just let it out as far as they can and slip it over their heads.

I know some who ask other people to tie their ties. Sometimes several at a time. These also stay tied forever.

The necktie manufacturers didn't miss the fact that normal men who drive trucks, cars, fly airplanes, operate complicated machinery, even computers, have trouble negotiating a necktie knot.

They now make ties that snap on, clip on, stick on, and ties that even zip on. Of course they cost more than the ones that have to be tied. But some men are eager to pay more just to avoid the hassle of tying a necktie.

Now I see more and more women wearing neckties. I don't see anything wrong with a woman wearing a necktie. If she wants to wear the most useless, most ridiculous piece of wearing apparel ever conceived, she has every right to. After all, men who know neckties are the most useless and most ridiculous piece of wearing apparel ever conceived, have been wearing them for years.

However, it makes me wonder which way the *Women's*

Movement is really going when I see a woman in a necktie.

I don't like neckties. I wear them occasionally because funerals, weddings, fancy restaurants, and other occasions require it. I can say proudly, however, that I've never worn a bow tie except when I've been required to wear a tuxedo.

The current issue of *Success!* magazine just bolsters my suspicions of people who do wear bow ties.

"The average person who wears a bow tie is distrusted by almost everyone," writes noted image consultant John T. Molloy.

I personally have never considered anyone who wears a bow tie average. But maybe the noted Mr. Molloy does.

He continues, "If you absolutely insist on wearing a bow tie, buy the proper accessories for it: a red nose and a beanie cap with a propeller.

"Attorneys traditionally avoid putting a bow tie wearer on a jury because bow tie wearers, they believe, are not likely to be moved by sound argument."

I don't know whether attorneys really believe this, as the noted Mr. Molloy says, but I know what I believe. I believe, if I were in court, I'd rather have a member of the jury wearing a red nose and a beanie with a propeller than one wearing a bow tie. I'd also want an attorney who could make a sound argument.

"The tie is the heraldic shield of 20th-century corporate America," says the noted Mr. Molloy. "The right suits and shirts are easy to pick because most are conservative and can camouflage a wearer's lack of clothes know-how. But ties give it away. The wrong tie on an executive or a would-be executive can be the bar-sinister of our day.

"The most useful tie by far is the rep—or diagonally striped—tie. It always sends the right message. To the most sophisticated executive, it announces that you are a member of his club."

I'm not sure I want to be a member of a club of sophisticated executives. I'm not much of a club man. I was a member of a club once, however, and I thoroughly enjoyed it. And you didn't have to wear the proper necktie to be a member.

The members did wear a special hat, however. And we had our own theme song. I still have my hat, although one of the ears has suffered severe closet damage. I still remember the words of the song, too. When I'm lucky enough to find an old Annette Funicello movie on television, I rush to get my hat and break into song. M-i-c-k-e-y M-o-u-s-e.

I wonder what the noted image consultant John T. Molloy would think of that.

I wonder. But I don't really care.

And Annette Funicello? She'd be just as gorgeous in a red nose and a beanie with a propeller.

38

And What About High-Heeled Shoes?

Martha Gerdeman, a former columnist and now a Dickson, Tennessee, English teacher, and I are engaged in a fashion debate.

She began a recent letter with, "Ever since Jerry Thompson moved into his Station, I have relished sharing his view of the world. Occasionally I may disagree with him; but for the most part, our opinions mesh, which proves that he's usually right."

Obviously a woman of superior intellect. I read on.

Referring me to a particular column, she said I managed to "make a totally absurd statement" when I said a necktie is "the most useless, most ridiculous piece of wearing apparel ever conceived." Additionally, I said I was amazed at why women now wear neckties.

"Sorry, Jerry," she continued, "but that is the voice of ignorance speaking. Any one of those women whose neckties amaze you could set you straight. The 'most useless, most ridiculous piece of wearing apparel ever conceived' comes in not one, but two pieces. Ask any woman and she will tell you that high-heeled dress shoes are both more useless and more ridiculous than neckties."

She pointed out that neckties are as useful as a Boy Scout's neckerchief. A Scout's neckerchief can be used as a sling, a tourniquet and for several other purposes.

"Now I ask," she said, "can high-heeled shoes save your life? Of course not. How many heroines have you seen get into really bad trouble in the movies because they were caught in the wilderness wearing high heels?"

I don't know about heroines, but I've covered stories involving men who got in trouble because they were caught on Lower Broadway wearing high heels.

Then she said, "Which brings us to another useful function of the necktie. It can be used to tie up a bad guy. Or it can be used to strangle an enemy. Just how would anyone commit murder with a woman's dress shoe, let alone tie up a bad guy?"

That question stirred my memory. In the early 1960s the city editor sent me down to a Printers Alley club to interview a woman at the bar.

I first looked up the clippings in the newspaper library about her past. I found several stories about her. One read, "A St. Louis businessman died in General Hospital today after being struck in the head with a high-heel shoe at a downtown night club. . . ."

So, Ms. Gerdeman, that's how you commit mayhem with a woman's dress shoe.

Now, let's get down to some real reasons for high-heel shoes. You say you have serious reservations about anyone who would sip champagne from a woman's shoe.

Not only is this romantic, but sometimes it improves the taste. I've had some champagne that would've tasted better from a sweaty old sneaker.

And you say you've been told high heels make a woman's legs look sexier. If so, you ask, why wear them with jeans?

It's not the shoes, it's the jeans that make the legs, and the rest of the woman for that matter, look sexy. Especially the new stretch jeans that fit so tight a woman can sit on a dime and tell whether it's on heads or tails.

Ms. Gerdeman, we could go on and on with this debate. But in the interest of conciliation, I'll concede that neckties *and* women's high-heel shoes are useless and ridiculous.

I'll also concede that you caught me. Yes, I sometimes do wear a necktie to work. But only in situations of impending crisis, so I'll have something to loosen.

And I like your scenario of my getting home after a hard day at the office. I say to Linda, "Boy, has Seigenthaler been mean to me today!" and she opens me a beer, loosens my tie, runs her fingers through my "fringe," and says, "Poor Baby! Sit down and relax and tell me all about it."

"Well, it seems that in my haste to get ready for work this morning, I mistakenly slipped on a pair of your chartreuse pumps. Can you imagine how they clashed with my pink tie?"

39

Runner's High?

I don't know what they are doing to cause it, but joggers are multiplying like rabbits.

Back when I first started practicing driving on rural roads, you had to watch out for too many rabbits. They would jump out from the roadside, from behind parked cars, from behind trees and shrubs. Now it's the joggers.

More than once I couldn't brake quick enough and we had hasenpfeffer rabbit for dinner. But you can't cook a jogger.

As the number of automobiles increased, rabbits understood that they were safer off the roads and streets. They kept to footpaths, woods and pastures. Not the joggers. They are everywhere. And at all hours.

Back when I was a police reporter, more than twenty years ago, any time you saw anybody running down the street you knew a cop or a jealous husband wasn't far behind. Now that was running for a purpose.

Today the people you see running down the street are running just to be running. It's purposeless. Worse, it's a form of masochism—which, according to Mr. Webster's famous book, is getting pleasure from pain.

Given my ample girth, I've been looking into jogging as one

of the methods of exercise when I finally go on my diet. I have done what the Vanderbilt professors call "empirical research." I have studied joggers closely, interrogated them seriously, analyzed them carefully.

Walk out your front door this morning, turn in any direction and within a minute or two you will be confronted by one or more of them. If it's a weekend you'll probably flush a covey of them.

Never will you see one in the act of jogging who is smiling with pleasure as he or she goes through this ordeal that he or she claims provides so much joy. They are intense about their runs. No jokes. Their faces are contorted with frowns and grimaces. Rivulets of sweat run the frowns that etch their tortured faces.

Every one I have ever seen in action looks like a Modigliani painting. Talk to them over a beer. They will tell you they love it. Whether they are mile-a-day hackers or marathoners, they have a vocabulary all their own.

They talk of their runs in weekly total miles. They discuss the relative merits of various brands of running shoes. They extol the virtues of a "runner's high." That's what they say they experience after they quit running.

Now that I can appreciate. I experienced it as a young boy. Papa's mule stepped on my foot. When the mule moved, it felt so good. It was a high all right. But even though I was very young, it taught me one thing that doesn't occur to most joggers who punish themselves day after day. You don't stand near the mule again just to feel another high.

I don't want to sound too critical of this pastime that has captured the free time of so many of my friends and fellow citizens. After all, joggers do make a significant contribution to the free enterprise system. I discovered that fact when I strolled—get that, I strolled, I didn't run—from the office to a downtown sporting goods shop to price a pair of sneakers and a pair of athletic shorts.

The nice saleswoman who waited on me was knowledgeable. You have to start, of course, with shoes, she said, and she recommended a pair that were on sale for fifty-five dollars. She told me if I waited until October a new "computerized shoe" will be on the market that will help joggers "interface" with how far they have run, how many calories they have burned and whether they are in their ideal running mode. That shoe will cost a mere one hundred twenty-five dollars.

I checked out some jogging suits. The one I liked was priced at one hundred thirty dollars. They didn't have my size. Linda suggested I try Nashville Tent and Awning Company if I was serious about it. At those prices, I wasn't very serious.

40

The Dangers of Chewing Gum

The number of gum chewers is growing, and some people aren't ready for it.

School teachers never will get used to gum chewers. I can see how it'd be disconcerting to see a room full of mouths working, but nobody talking.

Parents of young children aren't ready for it, either. They find chewed gum almost anywhere and everywhere. I've found it on my car seat. I usually make such a discovery just seconds after finding a wad on the seat of my pants.

I find it frequently on the soles of my shoes. I'm convinced that if a single wad of chewed gum was in the middle of a ten-acre field, I'd step in it. When I was a kid, I was always stepping in something else in the middle of a ten-acre field. But, believe me, that was easier to get off than chewing gum.

Chewing gum is obviously becoming more popular. Almost every time I turn on the television I see a beautiful set of twin girls urging me to double my pleasure. And just as my mind starts thinking of the ways, I realize they're talking about chewing gum. Other ads want me to use gum to brush my breath or clean my teeth.

Gum manufacturers constantly introduce new marketing

ideas. For years you could buy gum with baseball cards. Now they've added football cards, animals, cartoon characters and robots.

You can get it with sugar, or without. It comes in a variety of flavors ranging from tropical punch to watermelon. A couple of brands even enclose a drop of liquid in the center of each piece.

As soon as the so-called "smokeless tobacco" started gaining popularity, gum makers pounced on a new marketing technique. They started packing bubble gum in pouches like chewing tobacco or in small tins like snuff.

Suddenly, Joe and Matt were asking for gum in the tobacco-looking containers. My careful explanation that they were being gypped, that they could get more in a cheaper package, made no impact whatsoever. Hang the expense—they knew what they wanted.

The chewing gum concept has branched out into other areas. Now you can get gum that's supposed to cure sore throats and headaches. Gum to stop smoking. Gum to control your appetite. Gum to make "your breath kissing sweet." And gum to make you go to the bathroom.

My grandmother, "Great Mama" as we called her, loved to chew gum. She'd pick up a few packages of chewing gum in town every Saturday.

She was a polite gum chewer. She chewed silently with her lips together. And if she wanted to talk, she'd discard her gum in the woodbox or park it neatly on the tin can containing her snuff—depending on the chewing time.

Years ago, the mailman brought some free samples of Feen-A-Mint, a chewing gum laxative. She read the accompanying literature but didn't believe it.

"I know what a laxative tastes like," she said, almost defiantly, "and this tastes like chewing gum. That's all it is."

Great Mama liked the taste. She chewed several pieces. All went well until early the next day. Then things didn't go well, and they didn't go well with great frequency.

Great Mama suddenly would get a pained look on her face. Sort of a cross between disbelief, urgency, and incredibility.

Then she'd quickly drop whatever she was doing and move across the back porch with blazing speed. Within seconds we'd hear the hinges creaking on the outhouse. She'd covered the distance like a sprinter.

After several days of sprinting, Great Mama almost quit chewing gum. She did, however, take it back up later, but with considerable moderation. She never chewed more than a half piece at a time for the rest of her life.

And it just occurred to me the other day why. After the Feen-A-Mint, she never again found a piece of gum she'd trust.

41

Chain Letters

I wrote Monday about being lucky. I won a free Florida vacation that turned out to be anything but free.

But as luck would have it, there are some people out there who really want my luck to improve.

On the same day I won the vacation, last Friday, someone was mailing me a "good luck" letter. Another someone mailed me another "good luck" letter last Saturday. I got them both in Tuesday's mail. Neither was signed.

There are a few minor discrepancies in the two letters, basically in names mentioned, but otherwise they are identical.

They both start off with the phrase, "Kiss someone you love when you receive this letter and make magic."

Now that doesn't surprise me in the least. Kissing always makes magic. You can kiss someone you barely know. Or someone you've just met. Or a total stranger and magical things can happen. If you really want a dose of magic just kiss someone you hate, or someone you shouldn't. That has all kinds of possibilities, few of which, however, are associated with good luck.

Both letters also say they have "been sent to you for good luck. The original copy is in New England. It has been around the world nine times. The luck has now been sent to you. You will receive good luck within four days of receiving this letter provided you send it back out. This is no joke. You will receive it in the mail."

Several things really interested me about that first paragraph. First, why is the original copy in New England? Did it just land there on its ninth trip around the world? Or maybe it originated there and was just too good to let go.

Next, why was I singled out for this abundance of good fortune? I don't guess anyone can ever have too much good luck, but my luck hasn't been all that bad lately, either.

But what really puzzles me is how the letter writer can be so sure I'll receive this good luck in four days? Maybe it depends on how many people I kiss.

The letters instruct me to send twenty copies to people I think need good luck. Then it hit me with the biggest surprise of all. It instructed, "Don't send money, as fate has no price."

Somehow, I had expected from the first sentence that I'd come upon a plea for money. Something like sending a money order to the top name on a list while placing mine on the bottom. This "no money" concept is brand new to me.

The letters continued, "Do not keep this letter. It must leave your hands within 96 hours. An R.A.F. officer received $70,000. Joe Elliott (or Joe Bislet depending on which letter you take it from) received $40,000 and lost it because he broke the chain. While in the Philippines Gene Welsh (or Gen. Welch, another discrepancy) lost his wife six days after receiving this letter. He had received $7,755 before her death, but forgot to circulate the letter."

That settled it right there. I'm headed to the copy machine. It seems like so little when you compare it to losing your wife. But wait, it gets more convincing.

"Constantine Dias received this letter in 1953 (or 1958). He asked his secretary to make 20 copies and send them out. A few days later he won the lottery for two million dollars . . . Daleh (or Dain) Fairchild received the letter and not believing, threw it away. Nine days later he (or she) died."

That did it. I'm going to send them both out. I'll find 40 people who need some good luck. Maybe I'll send them to all the politicians who lost in last month's elections. Their luck could stand some improvement.

I even thought about sending one to Linda, but I changed my mind. She'd probably send it out and four days later I'd be run over by a Budweiser truck.

PART SEVEN

Friends and Heroes

42

A Real Hero

It's my contention that most real heroes become heroes by accident. They just happen to be in a situation that brings out their best.

Rick Blackburn found a hero. His hero was a janitor mopping the floor at St. Thomas Hospital. Blackburn offered the man a bribe and then skipped out without paying him. But he's still his hero.

Blackburn, the head of CBS Records in Nashville, is usually busy dealing with country music superstars. But, whenever time permits, he heads to the nearest tennis court. An avid tennis buff, he doesn't play just for the thrill of playing; he plays to win.

So, when he developed tennis elbow recently, he checked around and found that real athletes took an anti-inflammatory drug they claimed hastened their return to the playing field or tennis court.

So, Blackburn, who readily acknowledges he was "playing my own doctor," had to have some of the medicine. He convinced his doctor he needed this miracle cure for his bum elbow.

"I noticed an immediate improvement," Blackburn said. "I

would have patted myself on the back if my arm hadn't been too sore. I was looking forward to getting back on the court."

But before he was able to get back to his game, he suffered a setback that was life-threatening.

There's nothing funny about death or dying, but sometimes when a man thinks he's dying he will do funny things. Blackburn, now that he is recovered, can laugh at his actions when he was stricken.

He and his wife, Suzie, were eating at a Nashville restaurant when he began suffering excruciating pain in his chest.

"It was awful," Blackburn recalls. "It was intense pain in my chest and it burned like fire. As a stewardess, my wife had had some training in handling situations like this.

"I leaned over to Suzie and told her as calmly as I could, 'Don't panic or create a scene, but I'm having a heart attack. Get me to the hospital.'

"Well, she came close to betraying her panic training. I was all bent over as we left the restaurant. I was suffering severe pain. A fellow there said he had no idea the food was that bad. I didn't laugh.

"We get to St. Thomas emergency and they give me a lot of papers to fill out for insurance. I told them I didn't have time for the paper work, I was having a heart attack. Here I was playing my own doctor again.

"They insisted I fill out the papers. I started looking for a doctor. Suzie worked on the papers. I limped through a door that said 'Physicians only' and found this fellow mopping the floor.

"I remember telling him, 'Mister, I'm having a heart attack. There's $20 in it for you if you find me a doctor right now. If you don't. I'm going to die right here on your pretty, clean floor.'

"Within 30 seconds, that man had me a doctor and they were strapping me up to all kinds of machines. He saved my life. I'll never doubt it."

As it turned out, Blackburn was not suffering a heart attack. As a result of his first attempt at doctoring, the anti-inflammatory miracle drug he took for his tennis elbow irritated a small stomach ulcer he didn't know he had.

Finally the ulcer perforated, leaving a hole in the lining of his stomach. He underwent emergency surgery shortly after arriving at the hospital.

Blackburn now is back in his Music Row office on a restricted schedule and a more restricted diet. He's doing music and leaving the doctoring to doctors.

"I still want to find that janitor though," Blackburn said. "I owe him $20 and I'm going to pay him. He's a real hero.

"Meanwhile, we'll have to get together for lunch someday. You ever had Pablum? I'm getting it by the case."

Since I'm not sure I'll like it, I think I'll start with just a six-pack.

43

Death, Birth, Destiny

Reporters who cover street scenes have a funny way of recalling moments as flashbacks that are frozen in their memories like news pictures.

It was some time late in the war in Vietnam and I was watching a protest demonstration when I saw her—this grim-faced little lady walking along in the parade of picketers carrying a sign that read:

"It all balances."

Her face was somber, her expression unchanging.

All the other picket signs expressed strong sentiments against the war. Hers seemed ludicrous. It didn't make any sense.

"It all balances." I almost laughed when I saw it.

What did it mean?

Well, one day recently I finally came close to knowing. On that same day I visited two places I dread—a funeral home and a hospital.

The preacher at the funeral home didn't know Lola Page the way I knew her. He was a good preacher, I'm sure; but for my liking he read too much from the Good Book and said too little about this good woman I had known so well and loved so much.

While he was talking, my mind drifted over the many wonderful moments I had shared with this beautiful 91-year-old woman.

I first met Lola Page back in the 1960s. She was the grandmother of the woman I married. She became a grandmother of our son, Todd. She was old in years but forever young. She had a quick smile and a ready laugh.

I remember Sunday dinners at the church, the Rook games, the joking, the joshing, the sheer joy of being with her, talking to her, drinking in her wisdom and learning from it.

I remember returning from fishing trips with her husband, Raleigh. Always she rushed to inquire about our catch with great enthusiasm.

She knew that charity begins at home. I never heard her utter an unkind word about a single soul.

When our marriage went awry and ended in divorce, she didn't take sides or make judgments. She always was ready to profess her love for Todd and me.

I loved her so much I didn't want to go to her funeral, but I loved her too much to stay away.

After the burial I was moody and depressed. Later that day I visited the hospital, a bouquet in hand, for a new woman in my life. She was the newborn daughter of Phillips and Ginger Turner, Jr., who are good friends. What a woman! And what proud parents!

Phil's eyes were still filled with wonder and misty with emotion as he told me about the experience of being there during the delivery. I had personally known that experience.

There is nothing in this world to compare with the miracle of watching a newborn babe take the first breath of life.

My spirit lifted as I thought about Lauren Turner. Lola Page would have loved her.

So there is a beautiful old woman who has gone out of my life and a beautiful baby girl who has come into it. Life is renewed and replenished.

I hate losing my dear friend Lola who knew it was an

imperfect world. I love helping welcome my new friend Lauren into this same imperfect world.

And so for at least a little while the picket sign makes sense. It all balances.

44

A Perfect Test of Friendship

There's nothing like a fishing trip to cement a friendship. Or to test a friendship.

Not long ago, Ricky Shelton, a songwriter and singer, my dad, and I met my journalistic colleague, Robert Sherborne, in Leeville, Louisiana, for what promised to be an outstanding fishing trip. Dad doesn't like to fish, but he likes to travel.

Sherborne, my close friend, and I had fished there before. This time, we hoped to catch one we had never caught before— the bull redfish. Our Cajun friend, Ed Melancon, called a couple of weeks ago and told us "bull" redfish were running. Now, to be classified a "bull," a redfish must weigh a minimum of 14 pounds.

The first night there, Ed and his wife, Irma, took us to their isolated camp way out in the marshes. It's up on high pilings and power comes from a generator. We went across vast stretches of open, rough water in a pouring rain just to get there. We planned to have supper there and then net shrimp on the out-going tide. We took the shrimp for supper with us. Good thing, too. The weather turned nastier and the tide didn't move. The five of us were stranded all night in the middle of a Louisiana swamp—in a storm.

145

The weather was bad, but we were confident it would clear up. For three days it rained and the wind blew at about 30 knots. That alone is enough to test a friendship, but the ultimate test was still ahead for my friend Sherborne and me.

Finally, the weather broke on the third day. Within an hour we were catching fish. We had agreed to put $5 each in a pot for the one who landed the largest redfish.

About two hours later, Sherborne grunted, heaved back on his rod, and the battle was on. He had snagged the long-sought-after bull redfish.

Up to that point, Ricky was clearly going to take the money with a redfish that weighed just over six pounds.

Now it was obvious Sherborne had the prize on his hook and the money in his pocket if he could just get him in the boat.

The fight went on for five minutes. Then ten, then fifteen, before it became obvious Sherborne was winning the battle. We didn't have a landing net, so I put down my rod and rushed to help my friend. It seemed the natural thing to do.

After all, who was it that came to my rescue when I fell off the dock into the marsh, taking a pan full of shrimp with me to a watery landing? My friend Sherborne.

Who was it that bought the beer the next day? My friend Sherborne.

Who was it that challenged the female mud wrestling champion of Grand Isle to a match and then volunteered me to be her opponent? My friend Sherborne.

He convinced me that, win or lose, it would be a good column. Sherborne withdrew the challenge when he learned we'd have to pay for the mud.

Who was it that laughed hilariously with me the morning we heard Ricky practicing his Cajun dialect in the bathroom? You guessed it. Sherborne.

I had to help my friend even though it meant losing the bet. I reached over the boat as Sherborne brought the lunker alongside. As soon as I touched the line, it popped. The Great Bull Redfish went free.

I've never seen such a look of disbelief on the face of my

friend Sherborne. Then he spoke, "You . . . How could you do such a . . . thing? Of all the . . . rotten . . . dirty . . . lowdown . . . things you've done! How in the . . . could you do this . . . to me?"

I deleted all the expletives. I had never heard my friend use that kind of language.

Our search for the elusive bull red had ended. The passion for adventure had been drained. We headed for shore. Sherborne was sulking. Nobody was really smiling except that bull red deep in Lafourche Bayou.

A fishing trip is a perfect way to test a friendship.

But not the best way.

45

Chicken Billy

I've often heard it said there are two days a farm boy will always remember.

The first is when he finally decides to leave the farm and move to town. The second, and by far the most special of the two, is when he finally figures out a way to get back to the farm. I know the validity of this because I've personally experienced both.

My friend, Jack Hurst, has just recently returned to farm life. And he's taking to it like a tadpole takes to a muddy pond.

He was a little concerned, however, over whether his wife, Donna, would adapt to country living and even she admits a little apprehension. However, she's now a true convert. She's even raising a calf on a bottle. The calf's mother died from injuries suffered from a fall into a gully.

They live on a hilltop farm that overlooks Center Hill Lake. They grow vegetables in raised beds. They've adopted two stray dogs that have become family members. They run a small herd of Beefalo cattle and genuinely enjoy the pace of country living. It's a big change for them after living for a number of years in a Chicago suburb.

Jack, who writes a syndicated country music column for the

Chicago Tribune, is really getting into the new lifestyle. First, he cleared large areas by hand and built fences. Finally, he bought his first tractor and a pickup truck. It's a sure sign that a city boy is serious about country living when he buys a tractor and a pickup truck.

Jack also reads a lot. He reads farming publications and a variety of those books that relate enticing stories of city folk moving to a small farm and becoming self-sufficient. That appeals to Jack.

I talked with Donna last week. She'd just finished feeding the baby chickens. I remember growing up and seeing chickens in every yard up and down the road. Chickens are funny about that. They always go to the yard to rest when they're not in the garden pecking holes in the tomatoes or strolling across the front porch. Chickens look at front porches much like we look at banks. That's where they invariably leave their deposits.

I don't see many chickens in our community anymore. Supermarket chickens are much less trouble. And supermarket chickens come in all shapes and sizes. Some only have drumsticks, others just have breasts, and some just have thighs, but none of them have guts and feathers.

Donna said she and Jack decided to raise chickens to put in the freezer. She said Jack would do the slaughtering and she would do the freezing. Having known Jack for years, I'd say he might talk a good game of chicken slaughtering, but I'll have to see it to believe it.

In fact, I'll bet by next week, every chicken they own will have a name. And by the time they reach the age and size to slaughter, they'll probably be written into their wills.

Chicken killing is not a pleasant experience. I remember my grandmother wringing the necks off chickens. The headless birds would flop around in the back yard with blood spurting in the air until they finally quit moving. Then she'd briefly sock'em down in a bucket of boiling water and start picking off the feathers. Then it was time for the nasty part—gutting them. Hurst will never get through it.

While I'm not a person who likes violence, I do enjoy eating.

I told Donna to notify me when the Hurst chicken slaughter is scheduled. I want to be there. I can almost imagine what it'll be like.

"Now Jack, honey, be careful with Rosie here," Donna will say. "Do you remember how cute she was when she caught her first Junebug? And sweet little Norma. She was the one with the fuzzy tail feathers. Remember, we thought they'd never grow out? And there's Billy, and Susie, and Merle, and . . . Aren't they cute?"

And I can just hear Jack as he tosses aside his sharpened hatchet:

"Aw, hell, let's go get some barbecue. It's better with cold beer than chicken is anyway."

46

The Lord Sure Works in Mysterious Ways!

I've always heard it said the Lord works in mysterious ways and I've never doubted it.

Otherwise why would a single passenger survive a plane crash? Or why would a child submerged under icy water for more than 30 minutes be resuscitated? I have many personal experiences I can also offer as to the myserious workings of the Lord. Otherwise I wouldn't be here writing this column.

On the other side of the coin, however, I've known and heard about people who have religious experiences in some pretty strange places and under some pretty strange circumstances. I've even read that some people are more prone to call out for religion during sex.

I recall the space trip on which an astronant experienced a religious awakening. Upon his return to Earth, he left NASA and has since devoted his life to his religion.

A couple of the Watergate figures, Charles Colson and Jeb Stuart Magruder, had religious experiences that changed their lives after their convictions. Often we hear of prisoners "finding the Lord" while incarcerated.

Cousin Elmore did it in a more traditional way. He attended the Oral Roberts meeting at the fairgrounds many years ago and came away a changed man. A person who enjoyed strong spirits, Cousin Elmore served witness to the world he was changed, and then he denounced the evils of alcohol and offered himself as living proof of its destruction.

Everyone was so happy he'd changed. Two weeks later he changed back.

I've personally witnessed some of these transformations. I feel confident our daughter Niki had at least a mild religious experience when the bird got in the house and took a dive in her cake batter.

However, I'm convinced I witnessed Jimmy Murphrey when he had a strong religious experience. He shouted the name of the Lord. He yelled for God. He spoke in tongues, and he prayed. Several of his classmates besides me were there to see it too. It was a moving experience.

It all started when a farmer who lived near our school erected a small house at the end of his long drive. It was for the children of his tenant farmers to wait for the school bus in. It was very remote.

Constructed from heavy, rough cut, unseasoned oak, it must have weighed close to a ton. It sat solidly on railroad crossties.

Mysteriously, the house was lying on its side one morning. The farmer and his tenants got a tractor and some chains and righted it. Within a few days, the house had been upset twice more. The farmer was sick and tired of putting it back up. He put out the word he'd pay a large reward for information leading to the persons who kept turning it over.

Up to this point, I'd not been involved in these acts of wanton vandalism. Neither had Jimmy Murphrey. But somehow the offer of such a generous reward presented a challenge that just couldn't go unmet.

Six of us loaded in David Purdue's old Ford and drove to the little house late one Wednesday night. After driving around to make sure no one was watching, we decided to flip the house. We all lined up along one side and managed to lift it about two inches before someone shouted: "Here comes the law."

Quickly, we dropped the house and raced for the car. That's

when we heard Jimmy start preaching. In all my life I've never heard the words *God* or *Jesus* or *Lord* used as many times or said with such sincere emotion.

We'd dropped the house on Jimmy's little finger.

It was just another example of how the Lord works in mysterious ways. The sheriff wasn't in the neighborhood as we first thought. We didn't upset the house. And Jimmy Murphrey hasn't been the same since.

47

Suddenly, No Tomorrow

When I reported to work in the mailroom of the Methodist Publishing House in the 1950s, I was scared.

And I was anxious, and nervous, and all those things a high school student feels when starting the first real job.

There was another young man there doing the same thing I was doing—putting books in mail sacks. He was about my age, my size, but he'd worked there for a while before I came.

I noticed he laughed a lot, was always smiling, and had an unruly shock of almost red hair. At the first midmorning break we sat and talked. He knew I was nervous and scared. He told me which bosses to try to avoid and gave me some other pointers.

He worked across from me. A wide, never-ending conveyor belt ran constantly between us. The books came in an endless stream. If he saw me getting behind, he'd help.

Soon we became close friends. We had a lot in common. We both liked to work on cars. We liked fast cars. We liked old cars. And both of us could hardly wait until our temporary jobs in the mailroom were over. It was pure drudgery.

We began hanging around together after work and on weekends. His father owned a garage. We spent many Sunday afternoons puttering around the garage working on old cars. Once we managed to fit an Oldsmobile V-8 engine into a Ford Model-A chassis. Ole Henry Ford himself never envisioned the performance we got out of that old Model-A. After a couple of high-speed runs up and down a back road, the steering column dropped down in Ed's lap. His weld had failed.

We both laughed a lot about that. It was a nervous laughter because we both knew what would've happened had it broken loose just seconds before.

On another occasion I lost the end of a little finger when the trailer I was hitching up missed the ball and slid down the bumper. We'd planned to go camping. Instead, Ed drove me to the hospital where I got stitches and a skin graft. We even laughed about that later.

After that summer we didn't see a lot of each other for several years. I went on to college and Ed took over his father's garage.

I'd stop by occasionally, and we'd tell old stories and laugh. At one time we both were experiencing marital problems. We talked about it and found a lot of comfort in each other.

Not long ago I saw Ed on Old Hickory Boulevard. He was turning around in the driveway of a small church. I was in a hurry, so I just honked my horn, yelled and waved as I passed. He was smiling, as he always seemed to be, as he waved back.

I wish now I'd taken the time to stop and chat awhile. Sometimes we're in too much of a hurry. I did, however, make a mental note to stop by his garage in the next few days—when I had more time.

I was driving home on Sunday on Interstate 24 near Joelton when a police car passed me. The police car, with lights flashing and siren blaring, got off at my exit. I followed.

On Whites Creek Pike, at the Joelton exit, there'd been an accident. A small crowd was gathering. I pulled over, too. A woman was being treated for cuts and abrasions. A man, his head covered with a sheet, was lying near the guardrail. His head had been crushed by the wheels of his car after he and his wife were thrown from it.

They finally took the woman away in an ambulance, and

police continued their investigation before moving the man's body. I went to a nearby phone and informed city desk of the wreck.

It was later that Teddy Bart, on the television news, told me who the victim was. Bart blurted his name out in living rooms all over town: "A Nashville man killed this afternoon in a freak accident has been identified as Eddie Suddath, 44. . . ." I didn't hear anything else Bart said.

I looked at the missing end of my little finger, and my mind raced back thirty years.

I'm going to miss Ed a lot.

PART EIGHT

Saints and Hucksters

48

Sure, I Like Preachers

A while back some ministers of the gospel got upset with me because they interpreted something I wrote as being anti-preacher. Their letters and phone calls hurt my feelings.

The truth is that I believe in preachers, priests, rabbis, churches, religions, choirs—even the collection plate. But I also don't like what some ministers do sometimes.

I don't like preachers who constantly call for a return to prohibition as if they never heard the story of Jesus going to the marriage feast of Cana where they ran out of wine.

I don't like preachers who think they are acting out the social gospel when they lobby the legislature for bingo, against horse racing or lotteries—or in favor of forcing their view of the Bible on the public schools.

I don't like preachers who try to inflict heavy guilt trips on innocent children. Or on slightly less innocent adults. Granted, there are some of us hard-core sinners who need a little fire and brimstone from the pulpit on a Sunday morning. But that stuff—like manure in the garden out back—ought to be spread pretty thin.

I don't like preachers who think God is against women working as Her minister of Her word. Well, seriously, that's a

159

laugh-line Linda gave me. I'm not really sure about God's gender. But neither is any preacher who says he or she is sure.

And, finally, I don't like preachers who pretend that they and they alone have found It. They aren't preaching for salvation, but against tolerance. Against love.

But I like preachers who reach out to people who need it. Whenever I hear anybody say religion is a crutch, I think of all the people in this world who badly need somebody or something to lean on like the everlasting vine. That vine is more than a line in a hymn.

I like preachers who can stand in the pulpit on Sunday and make the gospel the good news. Lord knows we get enough bad news from the media.

I like preachers who practice what is preached and who teach as well as preach. I like preachers who make you feel you are a part of their congregation, even if you are just a visitor, who make the congregation feel it is an extension of the family and who make us feel we are all part of a larger family still.

I like preachers who live Love as well as preach it.

The truth is, I like most preachers I know. But I separate preachers from TV evangelists. TV evangelists aren't preachers; they are entertainers. They also are businessmen. I love to watch them entertain, but I wouldn't do a quarter's worth of business with them.

I love to watch the Swaggarts, the Angleys, the Bakkers, the Falwells, the Schullers, and the Robertses. They are fun to watch. They don't preach. They perform. You don't get the good news from them. You get the funnies. They are the comics of Christianity.

You haven't seen passion if you haven't seen Jimmy or Jerry call up the wrath of Satan on the humanists. You haven't seen pathos if you haven't seen Ernest or, in the old days, Oral, heal a diabetic of an excess of blood sugar. You haven't seen a variety show if you haven't watched Jim and Tammy Faye on the *PTL Club*.

Now Bob gives us a little more sophistication from the Tower of Power. I'd just like to have a percentage of their hair-spray concession. But as much as I enjoy their entertainment, I refuse to send them a thin dime to help polish the glass in the tower, or to buy a sheet for a bed in "God's medical school," or to get Jimmy's piano tuned, or Tammy's diamond polished, or Jerry's throat sprayed, or Ernest's tent patched.

49

Kids Need To Pray

The car zipped by me on the Interstate with a bumper sticker that said, "Kids need to pray."

I thought, what a great idea. Kids do need to pray. Adults need to pray, too. Then I thought some more.

What that bumper sticker really said was that the driver supported prayer in schools.

I remember praying in school, and I don't think it hurt me.

I went to a small country school, right across the road from a large Church of Christ. The minister was also my school teacher. A good one, too. I admired and respected him. Because I was raised a Methodist, I never heard him preach. But I heard him pray. A lot. We had prayer in the classroom every day.

We also had assembly every Wednesday where the Bible was read and someone prayed. It certainly never offended anyone. We were all of the Christian faith. Saying a prayer every morning right after the Pledge of Allegiance was a daily routine. We never thought anything about it.

Since then, I've thought a lot about it. What I think about it is not going to make me popular. That makes me feel bad. I like to be popular. I love to get letters from people who agree with me. I know most folks support prayer in public schools. *The*

Tennessean ran a poll several years ago that said three-fourths of the people in the nation favor prayer in public schools.

I don't expect to change anybody's mind. But we all ought to think about it.

Our children are our most precious gift. Their minds are our most precious resource. I think back to my own childhood. I wanted to feel a part of things. I was vulnerable. I could be hurt by other kids cutting me out of their circle.

If my ancestors had come to this country from the Far East rather than Great Britain, or if they had escaped persecution of the Jews, rather than persecution of Puritans, it is very likely my parents would have told me not to say a Christian prayer in school. I would have tried to obey them. And I would have been made to feel lonely, different and small. It would have hurt. It would have created conflict in the classroom with my friends and with my teachers. It ultimately would have caused conflict at home. Most of all, it would have created conflict in my mind.

No child should have to be punished that way.

Things have changed since I left that school. It now is integrated. There are also students of other faiths going there now—kids whose parents don't want their kids saying the prayers I prayed.

Linda and I have made certain our children know how to pray. If they are in school and feel a need to pray—before an exam, or before meals, or before a ball game—they know they can say a silent prayer.

But we don't want them to be part of anything that hurts even one child whose parents have taught them to believe differently than our kids.

We want them to know that praying is a personal thing between them and their God.

So prayer in schools is popular with politicians who forget that the people who settled this wild and untamed land risked their lives to escape religious persecution. They came here searching for freedom of religon.

Many died for that freedom. That's why we have it today.

And we must never take that precious freedom for granted.

I can pray anytime, anywhere I want, and to any God I want. So can my kids. So can yours, if they speak softly to their God. But it just isn't fair to make Christian kids say non-Christian prayers, or Jewish children say Christian prayers. Or Muslim kids. Or atheist kids.

After all, they are all God's children. God loves them all. Amen.

50

Could It Have Been Him?

Last Tuesday, someone shouted across the city room that there was a man on the sidewalk outside who claimed to be Jesus.

"Do you want to get a picture?" someone asked.

"No," the city editor answered with authority. "The guy is obviously crazy, and we're not in the habit of running pictures of crazy people."

There was something about this that troubled me. How do we know how Jesus would appear to people today? He'd probably look a little out of place wearing sandals, a long, flowing robe, long hair, and a beard. But that wouldn't necessarily make him crazy.

I suspect that Jesus was probably considered a little crazy when he walked the streets of Jerusalem almost 2,000 years ago. The Bible tells us he associated with prostitutes, lepers, money changers, and criminals. I suppose a person who did that today might be considered crazy. Or at least a little weird. For sure, someone who'd bear watching.

So, given the life I've lived and the fun I've had, I felt I couldn't take a chance. Who am I to say this man is not Jesus? I could at least go outside and talk with him.

165

He was wearing sandals, a long, flowing robe, and had long hair and a beard. He bore a strong resemblance to the pictures I've seen of Jesus.

I was not sure he was Jesus, but I was sure he was not crazy. Several things he said made sense.

"Many people who believe in Jesus," he said, "believe that this is me. Jesus came back the third time in a Greek body. And I have a new name. In Revelation three, verse twelve, it says I will put a new name on you. God's name is now Seuss.

"There are a lot of things that concern me. Ministers are telling us the end of the world is coming up soon. That was supposed to have happened in the days of the Apostles. In Matthew, it tells us about the tribulations; that the sun would darken and the stars fall from heaven. But it also tells us this generation will not go away until all these things take place.

"Do you want to say the world will be destroyed because Christ said it would? Or do you want to say Christ was a false prophet? Christ did not mean a literal destruction or a literal hell. I'm afraid we have people who are going to push a button and destroy the world just to prove a false prophecy.

"The kingdom, the heaven, the hell will be here on this earth. It will remain forever. Those taking care of their physical and mental body and treating their neighbors and other countries with respect will have peace. If you abuse your body, your mind, your neighbors, you will create your own hell.

"That's my message for the people of Nashville—people who are famous for publishing Bibles and pitching religion."

He carried a sign that said: "Nudist Christian Church, the humble road to heaven. God is naked also. Repent in the raw."

I asked him about this.

"The most humble state to be before God is to be naked," he said. "When you have no clothes on, you are not hiding anything. God doesn't like pretensions or masks. He wants you to be humble. God made us in his image. Look at a newborn baby. They're all born naked.

"I think every city should have a designated place to go naked. The Parthenon would be the perfect place here. Notice on top of the Parthenon. They have a large sculpture of a man with his genitals exposed. Isn't it the height of hypocrisy that they have a man in stone without clothes yet they outlaw human nudity?"

I couldn't answer that question.

I'm never going to miss even a remote chance to interview Jesus, but I'm not going to strip my clothes off in Centennial Park, either.

And just to be safe, I had him photographed. I hope to see him again and get it autographed.

51

Gospel Truth About TV Comedy

When it comes to television drama and comedy, don't give me primetime *Dallas* or *Dynasty* or *Falcon Crest* and don't give me Bill Cosby, Bob Newhart, or Red Foxx.

Give me the Sunday morning electronic church with the likes of Jimmy Swaggart, Ernest Angley, and Jerry Falwell.

Jimmy can make the devil seem more sinister than J. R. Ewing. Ernest can cure more ailments than Trapper John. And Jerry can put more guilt on you than *The People's Court*. And the commercials on the electronic church are slicker and quicker than that gang of beer-drinking rogues who run with Mickey Spillane, Rodney Dangerfield, and John Madden.

These commercials offer you religious booklets, plastic replicas of Jesus, an assortment of Bibles—some in living color—video cassettes, and salvation for your immortal soul. And all this for whatever price you think your immortal soul is worth.

One Sunday a while back I stopped by the newspaper and went into the conference room where there are three television sets side by side. Somebody had left all three sets on and there, all at the same moment, were Jimmy and Jerry, and some preacher conducting a Bible class—the holy trinity of electronic power. The volume was up on all three sets. Talk about the Tower of Babble. That was it.

Jimmy was sweating, and Jerry was looking sincere.

I turned down the volume on the sincere image and the Bible class and listened for a bit to the sweating Swaggart. He was shouting and the words ran together, but they sounded like, "You will repent your sins! Youwillrepent yoursins! Youwillrepentyoursins!" He said it about seven times, over and over. About the fifth time that he said it, the crowd started clapping.

He was so wrought up I started laughing at him. But the camera panned the audience, and everybody was stone-face serious, with some mouthing "Amen! Amen!"

When I tuned Ernest in, he was in the process of asking some stooped-over fellow with a cane exactly what ailed him. It was a bad case of arthritis. Suddenly Ernest slapped the man on the forehead and screamed "Hee-all!" The fellow jumped a foot off the floor and started bending over, touching his toes and doing kneebends. A miracle. Right in front of my eyes.

Again I started laughing. I kept right on laughing as he smacked a middle-aged woman who was suffering from "blood sugar" and cured her, then went to work on a deaf-mute he taught to say "baby" and "Jesus." It was miracle morning. I was chuckling. Ernest was chuckling, too. Maybe we both shared a joke.

Late in Jerry's show he went into his money pitch.

He wanted everybody to send him a check to help keep his Bible college going, to help his ministry, to help The Word go forth. He was talking in a soft voice, close to a whisper. He asked for any amount.

"Help keep our ministry on the air," he begged. I laughed out loud. His ministry isn't going off the air, and he knows it.

Later in the morning the electronic church featured the Rev. Robert Schuller and his Tower of Power, and Oral Roberts and James Robinson and the second version—on a different channel—of Jimmy Swaggart, and some other tithe-takers.

Ernest invited folks to spend their money with him on a trip to the Holy Land. Jimmy hustled a booklet that wouldn't be offered again—until the next time he offered it.

I went out of the room laughing like hell. Those guys are hilarious.

I don't plan to send them any money. When I give money, it's to preachers who visit the sick, marry couples in love, bury the dead, comfort the afflicted, and counsel the troubled.

I hope, however, that the rest of you keep sending money to the electronic church. I don't know what I'll do for laughs if they ever take those clowns off television.

52

Pastor by Mail

It seems that every time I decide not to write any more about preachers, another one pops up with a "message" I can't ignore.

The most recent one to come to my attention is also the most mysterious. He apparently doesn't appeal to his followers through radio or television. If he does, I'm unaware of it and unable to find out. Largely because I can't find him.

He is the Rev. Ewing. He signs his correspondence simply, "Rev. Ewing, Pastor by mail."

Virgil Frye, who lives in a Lafayette, Tennessee, nursing home, forwarded to me some of the mail he has received from Rev. Ewing.

The first letter, obviously computer-generated because it repeatedly referred to "Brother Frye," contained a packaged towelette such as you get from fried chicken restaurants. Rev. Ewing said it contained a "faith towel" soaked in "healing waters."

"I believe, Brother Frye," the letter said, "that God wants to open our eyes and show us where He wants us to be and how to get there, how to get under His spout where His blessings are pouring out . . ."

It then instructed Frye repeatedly to "USE THIS SEALED

171

FAITH TOWEL," and repeatedly referred to "St. John 9:7" in which "He touched my blinded eyes. Now I can see."

And just so Brother Frye wouldn't overlook it, and to make sure there was no mistake in its proper use, Rev. Ewing's missive, in large, bright red letters, instructed, "Here is how you're to use this sealed healing waters faith towel.

"Close your eyes and pray, 'Lord, let my spiritual eyes see You. And, Lord, show me where You want me.' Pray, 'Lord, I have to know where I am going in You so I will know when I get there.'

"Open your Healing Water (John 9:7) Faith Packet and take the wet towel out. With your eyes closed, just gently touch this Faith Towel to your eyelids.

"Next, wipe your billfold with this wet Faith Towel. If you have a checkbook, touch this Faith Towel to it.

"Lay $20.20, or $10.10, or $5.05 on top of this Faith Towel, wrap your $20.20, $10.10, or $5.05 inside this Faith Towel and pray, 'Lord, I am mailing this to Your work.' Then place it inside this envelope and get it back in the mail to the Lord. The church will pay the postage."

The next letter from Rev. Ewing was a dinner napkin with the outline of two hands on it. Rev. Ewing said they were his. If so, I bet Rev. Ewing is a funny looking little fellow because the hands outlined are not as big as our five-year-old's.

This letter instructed "Brother Frye" to "Go lay on your back and lay these Hands of Power over your face and whisper through these hands up to God what I tell you to in my letter. Then turn the napkin over and write me back. . . ."

Then what do you think it said? You guessed it:

"Please don't keep this sacred napkin. It is the key to your miracle. Then, by faith, lay your $20, $10, or $5 seed on this tracing of my hands as an act of faith. Fold up the $20, $10, or $5 as your faith seed in this tracing of my hands to help the church. Your giving this $20, $10, or $5 seed is so important to you. Then place the napkin in this envelope and mail it back here to me. . . ."

The postage-paid envelopes were addressed to Church and

Bible Study in the home by mail, c Rev. Ewing, P.O. Box 105278, Atlanta, Georgia, 30348. There is no telephone listing in Atlanta for Rev. Ewing or for the Church and Bible Study in the home by mail.

Virgil Frye, in forwarding this correspondence to me, told me he is more than 92 years old and knows "nothing of this kind of church."

Frye also said, "It's a scheme to chisel money from poor people."

That healing water must be powerful stuff. Brother Frye is seeing clearer already.

PART NINE

Surely You're Kidding!

53

Rooster Bingo

When it comes to making money, it goes without saying that some people are more creative than others.

Col. Harlan Sanders made millions frying chickens. He showed a lot of creativity with the way he blended his secret spices and cooked his chicken.

Benny Guillot, a New Orleans tavern owner, probably won't ever come close to making as much money as Col. Sanders, but he certainly may be as creative.

Guillot is already making money from the chicken business. But Guillot is not cooking the chickens. He's watching them poop.

It all started when business at his bar was as flat as the summertime chop on Lake Pontchartrain. It took a 350-pound Mississippian, Ed Gully, to get him back on the right track.

Gully noticed that Betty's Bar and Nora's Bar, both just down the road from Guillot's, were doing a lot more business. They were attracting patrons, including several they lured away from Guillot, by offering entertainment by oldies bands.

Gully had the idea to offer a different kind of entertainment at Guillot's. He constructed a large flat board with 100 numbered squares on it. Then on a Sunday afternoon, customers bought the squares for a dollar each. After purchasing their square, they all gathered around to watch what could be termed Rooster Bingo.

A little after three p.m., after all the squares had been sold, Guillot threw a chicken on the board and everyone waited for it to poop on one of the numbers. It was exciting. Especially for the person who held the lucky number because he collected the entire $100.

Thus the chicken drop was born and a transformation took place at Guillot's Bar. The crowds have been growing steadily since. On a recent Sunday, Guillot, sweat dripping from his brow, served the overflow crowd free fried fish and french fries. Later they had three chicken drops.

The bar has acquired three chickens. Guillot brags about them as if they were grandchildren.

"We got the Brown Bomber," Guillot says proudly. "He's a big Rhode Island Red Rooster that really puts on a show. Then we got the Big Boomer. Those two are really the good ones. The third one is Fran. She's real slow so we named her after one of our waitresses."

I was glad to hear about this place. And about the chicken drop. You see, I know how to make my chicken win everytime.

It goes back to my childhood on the farm. Willie Biggs, an old black man who sometimes helped my grandfather, showed me and my brother Ronnie how to hypnotize a chicken.

It was pretty simple. All you had to do was to catch a chicken and cross its legs. With the legs crossed you sat it down in a dusty space and drew a circle completely around its body.

The chicken would stretch its neck to watch you draw the circle. But once it was completed, the chicken was mystified. While it kept looking at the circle, it wouldn't move until you dusted away part of the circle. Then it would jump up and run off.

To test Willie's method, Ronnie and I took out a can of chicken feed one day and lured all my grandmother's chickens up to the trough. Within a few minutes, we had the whole flock hypnotized. The only thing moving was their necks.

We were so proud of our mass effort, we went to get our grandmother to show her. When she saw all the chickens lying on the ground, her only comment was, "Lordy mercy, they've all got the limber neck. They'll be dead by dark."

Ronnie and I thought this was pretty funny. That is, until we showed her the chickens were really all right. We borrowed her broom and started brushing out the circles. One by one the chickens got up and ran off.

When we gave her the broom back, it was our turn to run off.

I hope I get to Guillot's before he expands to a cow drop. I don't know how to hypnotize a cow.

54 _____

"Hey, Old Buddy"

A few weeks back my publisher wrote a column in which he admitted that he ducks and dodges bums and panhandlers.

Not me. I love a good story, and there are some creative dramatists out there on the streets.

I listen, grade their stories, and give them a little change.

"Old Buddy," they often begin. When you hear "Old Buddy," you know it will be a direct, not a subtle, approach.

The other day I was leaving my car in a downtown parking lot when two of them, a man and a woman, stepped in front of me.

The man was somewhere between 50 and 75 years of age. Given the grit and grime in his whiskers, it was hard to judge.

I perceived that the person with him, sans whiskers, was a lady. My mother taught me not to guess ages of females.

"Old Buddy," he began, "my wife and I are trying to get bus fare to Watertown to see our baby boy. He is real sick, and we need to get there quick. Could you help us out?"

The woman dabbed at her eyes with a stained bandana. The facial dirt didn't smear; she was dry-eyed.

"He's sick, sick, sick!" she sobbed. I assumed she was talking about their baby boy, not the man with her.

I guessed that baby's age was probably around 34. But, what

SURELY YOU'RE KIDDING! • 181

the heck, I made a mental note to give him a B-minus and dumped coins in his hand.

He profusely thanked me on behalf of Baby.

Later, I had another encounter with a bum. "Hey, Old Buddy!" He was leaning against the building at West End Avenue and 18th as I walked by.

"I haven't had a bite to eat since yesterday morning. I'm starving. I'm so weak from hunger I can't take another step. Could you spare a little change?"

I don't know when he had eaten last, but from his aromatic breath I could tell he was not dying from thirst. All the stories about world hunger, and here it was at home. I gave him a quarter—and a solid C.

There also is the subtle approach. On Union Street, he was standing across from the Tennessee Performing Arts Center, staring up toward the horizon.

"I hope she doesn't jump," he said to me. I took the bait like a trout going after a dry fly.

"There was a redheaded woman on the roof looking over, but she's gone now."

I then felt the sting of the hook; I already had the bait in my mouth.

"I can tell you care about people," he said. Suddenly, I knew. "I need a handout, brother. Can you spare a little change?"

It was slick. I had given him the money, and he was gone while I was still looking for the redheaded woman. B plus.

As I came out of the courthouse, the two fellows nailed me as I waited for the light to change.

"Sir?" No "Old Buddy" from these two. They didn't look hungry, but they walked a sort of stumble-shuffle.

"Sir," the tall one began. "Would you do me a favor?"

"Well, I'm about broke," I said in anticipation, "and I'm trying to find somebody to buy me a cold beer."

"Oh sir," he said, "you've got me all wrong. I've got money. See here?" Mutt reached in his pocket and pulled out a rumpled dollar bill and some coins.

"I wish you would give my little buddy here some money.

He's broke, and he's bugging the hell out of me to give him some of mine and I ain't gonna do it." An A. Barely. But an A.

I handed Jeff some small change and laughed out loud. The stories in the streets beat soap operas.

55

A Warm Night Downtown

There are times when I have to do something different in order to perform the normal routine. It happened this week.

Tuesday night I was trying to write. It seemed I was walking backwards. I had to do something different. I had several choices. I could visit in the sports department, go home, go get a cold beer, take a walk, or not write at all and start looking for another job.

As soon as I stepped out the front door, I decided to walk. Less fattening than a beer. More interesting than the sports department. It was balmy outside.

Warm weather brings out more than a hefty columnist. Young kids were playing and laughing on the parking lot of McDonald's across the street. Eighth Avenue North was teeming with people. Teen-agers around the door of Hume Fogg High School. An older crowd at the Classic Cat. Two young street toughs in a doorway near Commerce:

"Hey, man," said the shorter one, "how about 40 cents for a beer?"

I answered with a question of my own:

"Fellow, if I knew of a place serving 40-cent beer, do you

think I'd be wandering around out here on the street?"

"Well, how about a cigarette then?"

"I don't smoke."

Less than a block farther on, I was stopped by a fellow with bushy black hair and a distinct foreign accent. He was looking for a particular bar. The address he had was in the near vicinity, but I'd never heard of the bar. Something like the name of a man and woman. He understood me better than I did him.

"Do you live near here?" he asked in broken English.

"Yeah, just down the street," I answered. Why try to explain? Telling him I lived in Coopertown would have just added to his confusion.

I did try to help him find the bar.

"Do you know anything about this bar?" he asked.

"No, I've never heard of it."

"Are you gay?"

Suddenly, I knew why I'd never heard of it.

Warm weather brings out hookers, too. There were three on the corner of Eighth and Church Street. Two were rather attractive. But it would have taken at least a couple of six packs for the third one to start getting any prettier.

Then there was the fellow with the guitar walking up and down Lower Broadway. Said he hoped some club would let him sit in with the band. I hope one did.

The doors to the beer joints were standing open. Different songs, in different keys, were coming from each. People milled around on the sidewalks. Fourth and Broadway was especially interesting. An adult bookstore on one corner. A club with dancing girls on another. And on another, The Resting Place, where they preach and sing hymns. And where they don't allow alcohol. Or country music.

My trek back to the paper took me by the Southern Baptist Convention. There, a lone picket walked back and forth in front of the building. Sporting a mottled gray beard, he wore a sandwich board urging the "SBC Ex. Comm." to "please give me 10 minutes of your time."

I thought he might be an interesting interview.

"Having any luck?" I asked.

"I'm still walking, aren't I?"

"Have any members of the executive committee talked with you?"

"You a Baptist?"

"Nope, I'm a newspaper writer. You just talk to Baptists?"

"I'll be taking a break about 8:30."

At first I started to wait. It was just a few minutes away. Then I wondered why should I spend my time waiting on a man begging someone else for their time? Two reasons came to mind: One, his mission was probably deeper and more weighty than I wanted to deal with. And two, the hookers were friendlier.

Yep, warm nights sure bring out a variety of people.

Maybe next time, I'll go for the cold beer. Or lie about being a Baptist. Or both.

56

Quick Release Britches

I was surrounded by dozens of attractive women, all worked up to a sexual frenzy.

They were screaming, panting, squirming, gyrating, yelling. They were shouting "take it all off."

The beer was cold. The music stimulating. For a fleeting instant, I thought I was in heaven.

Wrong.

The women were all good looking, all right. They were obviously worked up, too. And they were yelling for men to take their clothes off. Problem is none of them knew I was there.

They were screaming for the male strippers who performed Thursday at Sal's Club to take off their clothes. And they were not disappointed.

This was the second Nashville appearance of the Heavenly 7, an all-male revue produced by Daryl Madden. The first was a month ago, also at Sal's at I-24 and Haywood Lane. Both shows were sellouts.

The show was under way when I got there. A fully clothed man was swaying to the beat of the music. The women responded loudly to every move. He tantalized them by opening the top of his shirt ever so quickly and then closing it. The volume of the screaming women rose and fell proportionately.

Finally, after much teasing from the man and even more urging from the women to "take it all off," he shed the shirt.

Then he unzipped his tight pants. The women screamed. He pulled the zipper back up. They booed. The process was repeated several times.

As the audience response reached a fever pitch, the dancer turned his back to the crowd. Gyrating wildly, like a hula dancer with her grass skirt on fire, he leaned forward.

In one split second, one quick move, one loud gasp from the women, the man snatched off his pants.

The women were obviously impressed with his briefest of briefs underneath. I was impressed by his quick-release britches.

The women loved it. Now they were making suggestive moves. They called the dancer to their tables. They waved money in the air.

He responded. He danced among the tables. On tables. On a railing.

Everywhere he danced, the women stuffed money in his drawers, moving their hands and various other body parts up and down his naked torso. Meanwhile, his drawers grew fuller. So full, in fact, that he had to remove a large wad of the money and hold it in his hand.

Madden, dressed in a shiny silver suit, served as master of ceremonies. The women kept yelling for him to take his clothes off. He refused. Instead, he'd introduce the next act.

The acts included a dancer who appeared drunk. Dressed like a shabby wino, he staggered to the stage from the crowd. Within minutes he, too, had snatched off his britches and the women were stuffing his drawers with dollars.

Then a Metro policeman went to the stage and told Madden he was under arrest. At least I *thought* it was a Metro cop. He had on a uniform, a Metro shoulder patch, a nightstick, handcuffs.

I thought it was a raid until he started dancing and the women started screaming. I wasn't real sure until he popped off his quick-release britches.

As the "policeman" danced, a voice overrode the music, "Now ladies, don't try this on the street. This man has been properly trained for this duty."

The grand finale brought all the male performers to the stage for a group dance. Madden even got the spirit and removed his britches.

Once the show was over, the women left quickly.

I left too. But I left with a serious intention to get me a pair of quick-release britches. At my age, a fellow doesn't have any time to waste.

And besides, women might stuff money in my drawers to get me to put 'em back on.